ETERNAL DAY

THE FAITH SERIES

THE FAITH
Understanding Orthodox Christianity

THE WAY
*What every Protestant Should Know
about the Orthodox Church*

THE TRUTH
*What Every Roman Catholic Should Know
about the Orthodox Church*

THE LIFE
The Orthodox Doctrine of Salvation

ETERNAL DAY

*The Christian Alternative to
Secularism and Modern Psychology*

Seth Farber

REGINA
ORTHODOX PRESS
SALISBURY, MA

1998

ISBN 0-9649141-3-1

Printed in Canada

All Scripture quotations are from the King James Version unless otherwise noted. Some quotations have been emended by the author to better reflect the original Greek text.

Seth Farber, Ph.D.
172 West 79th Street
Apartment #2E
New York, NY 10024
(212) 799-9026

Regina Orthodox Press
P.O. Box 5288
Salisbury, MA 01952
1-800-636-2470
FAX: 978-462-5079

The Lord's Day is great and glorious. The Scripture
knows this day without evening, having no other day, a
day without end. . . . Whether you call it a day or an age it
is all the same.

St. Basil the Great

This day which concludes the history of salvation, the
day of victory over the forces of evil . . . is the beginning
of the New Aeon.

Father Alexander Schmemann

CONTENTS

INTRODUCTION

This book will attempt to demonstrate that psychology's claim to be a value-free scientific discipline is spurious; I will argue that it constitutes instead a religion of sorts, a rival to Christianity. The practical goals of this book, stated negatively, include motivating Christians to stop referring persons who are experiencing emotional distress to mental health professionals, and to cease attempting to integrate Christianity with current psychological and psychiatric theories. The positive goals of the book include enabling readers to realize that the Christian faith and community are more powerful tools for healing and transformation than the mental health system, and inspiring Christians to establish alternative places of asylum for individuals who are undergoing spiritual-emotional crises.[1]

In order to make these goals attainable, one must first establish a theoretical foundation for what will undoubtedly be an unfamiliar form of practice, albeit similar in

---

1   The Bishop of Nafpaktos Hierotheos Vlachos has written two eloquent books on "Orthodox psychotherapy," with which I disagree. There is much of great value in these books on mystical contemplation and ascetic self-discipline, but he implies an individualized eschatology that I have rejected (see Prologue and Chapters 9, 11 and 14), and I believe his anthropology is seriously compromised by his reliance on the root metaphor of man as diseased. See Archim. Hierotheos Vlachos, *The Illness and Cure of the Soul in the Orthodox Tradition* (Levadia, Greece: Birth of the Theotokos Monastery, 1993) and *Orthodox Psychotherapy* (Levadia, Greece: Birth of Theotokos Monastery, 1994). This is antithetical to the self-understanding of the early Church, which emphasized the Christian's strengths and gifts. (See, for example, St. Paul in Ephesians 4:8-13.) See also Chapters 11-14 below.

many ways to that of the early Church for the first two centuries after its inception. This book begins with an examination and critique of the philosophical perspective that is often presented as "Christian," but which I contend derives not from Christ or the New Testament but from the later Augustine (dating from the time he wrote *The City of God*).

This perspective consists of a deep structure of philosophical, theological and crypto-theological assumptions that have shaped religion, Western culture, and psychology for centuries—in other words, they are at the root not only of religious but of modern secular schools of thought, whose adherents pride themselves on their distance from the past with its burden of anachronistic superstitions.

I argue that this deep structure of assumptions constitutes an ontology of deficiency,[2] of flaw, which posits a lack in the depths of the ontological heart of the universe. Translated into theological terms, it depicts a God whose love or grace is not sufficient to encompass all of creation and who wills that a large percentage of humanity suffer eternal torment in Hell. The consequences of accepting such an ontology/theology have been catastrophic, engulfing humanity in an atmosphere of doom and death for

2   Ontology is the branch of philosophy that is concerned with the nature of reality, of being, of existence. I will argue that there are fundamentally two schools of thought about the nature of existence. I will use a variety of metaphors to characterize the ontological position being described (mostly drawn from the primary sources themselves), because these metaphors have subconscious resonances that one must take into consideration when attempting to understand an ontological position—to feel its texture. An ontology inexorably has an evaluative dimension. For example, if reality is "deficient," then it is lacking in worth, in value.

10

centuries, making it impossible to perceive and respond to the infinite and inexhaustible grace of the Father of Jesus, and obscuring the vision of the realization of the Kingdom of God on earth.

The alternative to the ontology of deficiency is an ontology of sufficiency, which posits an infinite plenitude in the heart of being. Such an ontology was posited by Jesus, who expressed it in theological terms as the infinite grace of the Father, who eagerly welcomes the prodigal son home, wills that all sinners accept His offer of redemption, and attempts through Christ to inaugurate the Kingdom of Heaven on earth.

More specifically, the Prologue attempts to establish the eschatological nature of Christianity—that the Kingdom of God is the object of Christian faith. Parts 1 and 2 of this book explicate the ontology of deficiency as it is presented respectively by Augustine, Luther, Calvin, Freud, and Freud's contemporary epigones—and in a modified form in biological psychiatry.[3] I argue that all the myriad

3   Unlike contemporary Protestant and Catholic scholars, Orthodox thinkers have not been reluctant to criticize Augustine (or Luther and Calvin). Glenn Tinder's trenchant critique of Augustine in the conservative Catholic journal *First Things* is hopefully a sign that Catholics (and Protestants?) are beginning to acknowledge the baneful effect some of Augustine's doctrines have had upon society. (See Glenn Tinder, "Augustine's World and Ours," *First Things*, December 1997, No. 78, pp. 35-43.) Clark Pinnock is one of the strongest critics of Augustine from within the evangelical Christian camp. See, for example, *Tracking the Maze* (San Francisco, California: Harper and Row, 1990) p. 192, and *Unbound Love* (Downers Grove, Illinois: InterVarsity Press, 1994). For explicit critiques of Augustine by Orthodox thinkers, see John Meyendorff, *Catholicity and the Church* (Crestwood, New York: St. Vladimir's Seminary Press, 1983) and

ontologies/theologies since Augustine have been influenced in different ways by the core Augustinian premise that there is an unbridgeable abyss between God and humanity or—to put it in secular terms—between nature and humanity.

Chapter 9 critiques the various rationales Christians have given for delegating the spiritual care of souls to the mental health system. (Obviously this care or "mental health treatment" is really destructive.) I argue that Christians have credulously accepted the positivistic scientific-expertise claims of mental health professionals and have failed not only to scrutinize the philosophical premises on which various psychologies have been based, as I did in the preceding chapters, but to intellectually engage (or even familiarize themselves with) the writings of those who have trenchantly critiqued the mental health system (or the human services in general) in the last few decades.

This chapter is influenced by my reading of neo-Anabaptist theologians (as well as Eastern Orthodox to some degree) who have argued that Christians have become enmeshed in and coopted by power structures they originally entered with the hopes of transforming. (This is

Alexandre Kalomiros, "The River of Fire" (*The Christian Activist*, Winter/Spring, 1997, Vol. 10). See Frank Schaeffer, *Dancing Alone: The Quest for Orthodox Faith in the Age of False Religions* (Brookline, Massachusetts: Holy Cross Orthodox Press, 1994), pp. 63-92, for a modern Orthodox's unflinching critique of Augustinianism and its historical consequences. He writes, "The Orthodox East has at its core an understanding of a mysterious, loving God. In the Augustinian West a vision of a juridicial vengeful, capricious god-devil emerged [during the Reformation] leading in the end to a rebellion against religion altogether" (pp. 71-72). See also the quotes from various Orthodox philosophers dispersed throughout this book.

precisely what has occurred with the "Christian psychology" movement.) Thomas Finger wrote, "In my view...the Church impacts this world not chiefly by seeking to help its present structures to function better, but by presenting it with new alternative possibilities."[4] Finger and others argue that only to the degree to which we live wholly in the light of the "age to come" can the world be overcome and the Kingdom of God take shape as a "recognizable and concretely possible option."[5] Only then can the Christian community exist both as an "alternative society" and a "transformative example."[6] I call upon the Orthodox Church to take leadership in establishing alternatives to the "mental health" system.

Chapter 10 attempts to show that "schizophrenia" is a social construction maintained by psychiatry in alliance with a number of other industries that have economic, political and other motives for continuing to manufacture mental patients and other enfeebled individuals who are the recipients of their products and "services." The second part of this chapter is based on my conclusion that schizophrenia is a death-rebirth experience that could potentially be a prelude to accepting a new identity as a disciple of Christ. I urge readers to understand the implications this reality has for Christian missionary endeavors.

4   Thomas Finger, *Christian Theology: An Eschatological Approach, Volume 2* p. 289. Most Anabaptists (as do most Protestants) use the term *Church* to refer to all Christian denominations, whereas many Orthodox use it to refer exclusively to the Orthodox Church. Unless otherwise noted in the text, the reader can assume that when I quote or paraphrase an author, this pattern of usage is being followed.
5   Ibid., p. 294.
6   Charles Scriven, *The Transformation of Culture* (Scottdale, Pennsylvania: Herald Press), p. 181.

In Chapters 11 through 14 I develop an alternative ontology/anthropology to that of modern psychology and other secular schools of thought. This perspective developed out of my readings of theologians and philosophers within the Eastern Orthodox tradition who explicitly or implicitly rejected the premises of Augustinianism. I argue that the transcendence of Augustinianism, as well as of secular humanism, and the commitment to an ontology of plenitude and a Christian humanist anthropology is a precondition for overcoming the hiatus between God and humanity and thus for accepting God's invitation to pass through the gates of paradise and to rebuild the heavenly city of Jerusalem upon the earth.

Although I write out of an Orthodox context, this book is addressed to all Christians, and indeed to individuals of other faiths as well, who suspect or believe that modern psychological and psychiatric theories do not illuminate the human situation and that the mental health system (and other human service institutions) is not providing genuine solutions to the problems of contemporary life.

ACKNOWLEDGEMENTS

My intellectual/spiritual debts are evident from the sources cited in the book—and from my dedication. I will single out for mention here R.D. Laing, the British psychiatrist.

I am indebted to my friend Frank Schaeffer for his commitment to my project—after so many other supporters jumped ship when they (belatedly) realized I was knowingly heading into the turbulent waters of controversy—as well as for his excellent editorial recommendations.

The support of my parents was indispensable, as was the friendship of Hardina Dahl. Others who contributed emotionally or spiritually include Deniz Tekiner, my sister Patricia Martinez, and her family, Father David Kossey, Ray Russ, Franklin Greewald, Pasquale Galante, Larry Simon, James Mancuso, Norman Kraus, Laura Woodruff, Danielle Deschamps, Leonard Frank, Charles Dennis, and Bishop Seraphim Sigrist (editor of *The First Hour*).

ABOUT THE AUTHOR

I am a psychologist and an opponent of the mental health system, a Christian and a member of the Orthodox Church. I was raised in a secular Jewish home in New York City, baptized by a Baptist minister in 1991, and chrismated into the Eastern Orthodox Church in 1994.

In 1976, when I was twenty-four years old, I decided against continuing acting or high school teaching and entered the New School for Social Research to pursue graduate studies in psychology. I transferred schools several times for various reasons, and completed my doctorate in 1984. At that time I was a devout believer in the Freudian religion. There was only one crack in my Freudian faith: I was fascinated by "schizophrenics," and believed they suffered from a curable disorder. In other words, I rejected the dogma common to mental health professionals of virtually all schools—and contested by psychiatric heretics Thomas Szasz and R.D. Laing—that schizophrenia is either a *chronic mental* disorder or a *brain* disease.

My doubts about Freudianism grew stronger in 1984. I became uncomfortable regarding my clients as "mentally ill" rather than as human beings contending more or less successfully with the problems of life. After studying theory and therapy with two of the pioneers in the family therapy movement, I completely rejected the idea of mental illness. I now believe that those who are labelled mentally ill are responding to real—and usually unacknowledged—conflicts in their social context (which usually includes the nuclear family).

In 1988 I met George Ebert, who had been an activist in the mental patients rights movement for close to fifteen years. In the mid-1970s he was diagnosed as a chronic schizophrenic after he had a "nervous breakdown." Ebert proved the system wrong: He is today, as he was when I met him, a vigorous advocate for psychiatrically-labelled persons, who runs a government-funded crisis center. He is happily married—by now it must be close to thirty years—and the father of two grown sons. At his suggestion I formed The Network Against Coercive Psychiatry, an organization committed to opposing the crimes against humanity committed by the mental health system (see Appendix 2). As a result of the public relations work I did on my own, I appeared in the late 1980s and early 1990s on a number of television shows (*Geraldo, Oprah Winfrey,* William Buckley's *Firing Line*) and radio programs in an effort to expose the myths promulgated by the mental health system. In 1993 my book *Madness, Heresy and the Rumor of Angels; The Revolt Against the Mental Health System* (Chicago: Open Court, 1993) was published with a foreword by Thomas Szasz. The book tells the (true) stories of seven individuals who had "breakdowns," were labelled "schizophrenic" or "manic-depressive," and "recovered." Their recovery was a result of the fact that they eventually rejected the advice of their psychiatrists, gradually weaned themselves off psychiatric drugs, completely extricated themselves from the mental health system and its various institutions, and went back to work or to school.

As a result of my book and my media appearances, thousands of individuals have called or written to me describing their abuse by the mental health system, asking for advice, or telling me their success stories. I have spoken to several hundred persons who had breakdowns, were labelled mentally ill, and proved the mental health system wrong by successfully resisting professionals' efforts to induct them into careers as chronic mental patients.

I think that my own refusal to be inducted into the role of a mental health professional stems in large part from a spiritual quest I began in the early 1970s that inspired me with a expansive vision of human possibility as opposed to the cramped vision of mental health professionals. This *quest* reached a culmination with an experience of God I had in 1989 and has now been transformed into a spiritual *mission*.

In the 1980s I read and re-read the works of the Indian philosopher Sri Aurobindo. Aurobindo did not accept the Platonic-Hindu idea that the quest for happiness and liberation can only be attained when one is freed from the body. He was a witness for the possibility of the divine life on earth. He wrote, "The ascent of man into heaven is not the key, but rather his ascent here into the spirit and the descent also of the spirit into his normal humanity and the transformation of his earthly nature. For that and not some post-mortem salvation is the real new birth for which humanity waits as the crowning moment of its long, obscure and painful course."

In 1990 I discovered that the same kind of vision articulated by Aurobindo was at the heart of the "mystical theology" of the Orthodox (Christian) Church.[7] In 1994 I considered joining the church but temporized. I took the plunge in April 1994 after an exchange of letters with Philip Sherrard. Sherrard stated that I might be right, that the Church might be too "sclerotic" (my term) to launch an offensive against psychology and secularism. But "I don't

7   See Vladimir Lossky, *The Mystical Theology of the Eastern Church* (Crestwood, New York: St. Vladimir's Seminary Press, 1976).

see that the situation is not far worse when it comes to launching such an offensive outside the Church. Who is going to do it, and in the name of what? The devil cannot cast out the devil. To say that every institutionalized form of the Church is now in the hands of the devil would be to say the Holy Spirit no longer manifests Himself through any such form....Ultimately the sole standard is holiness; I would have thought one has to be very cautious before one affirms that there is no manifestation of holiness among those who participate in the liturgical and sacramental life of the 'visible' Church and if there is such a manifestation, then the Church is not in the hands of the devil, but God is operative through it. And where God operates anything can happen!"[8]

Sherrard's optimism about the Church has been corroborated by subsequent events. It is notable that this book was originally contracted with a non-Orthodox publisher who later decided against publishing it. It strikes me as providential that Regina Orthodox Press is now the publisher.

People are frequently surprised that I, a psychologist, am such a passionate opponent of the mental health system. I believe my zeal stems in large part from my vivid sense of mission. As I wrote in 1990 (in a letter to a mental patient who solicited my advice):

> Because I have the social credentials, the knowledge, the wisdom, and because I have been granted the grace to see clearly what is happening, I could, given the opportunity, expose to the American public the lies of the Mental Health Establishment and rekindle the hopes

8   Personal correspondence, January 15, 1996.

and dreams of those who have been downtrodden and dispirited by the Psychiatric Priesthood.

I have trembled in fear before the sense of awesome responsibility that lies before me, before us. But I believe it is my mission to help undermine the power of the modern day Pharisees (the Psychiatric Priesthood) who seek to bar the gates of heaven to those they have been trained to despise. I know how vast and ominous is the shadow of death that lies across this nation and that turns millions of gentle souls into servants of fear. But I know also how bright, how glorious, is the promise of salvation—if only we have the courage to open our eyes. I know that God's love for us is boundless, infinite—if only we have the trust and the humility to receive it.

I hope to talk with you again soon.

Sincerely,

Seth

PROLOGUE

But seek first the Kingdom of God....
Matthew 6:33

Our Lord left to us His own work to carry on and to accomplish. We have to enter into the very spirit of His redeeming work. And we are given power to do this. We are given power to be the sons of God.
Georges Florovsky[9]

The crisis of Christianity, I am convinced, is not that it has become irrelevant to the world—for in a way it always remains "scandal to the Jews and foolishness to the Greeks"—but that the Kingdom of God, as value of all values, the object of its faith, hope and love, the content of its prayer "Thy Kingdom come!" has become irrelevant to Christians themselves.
Father Alexander Schmemann[10]

According to Schmemann, one of the most prominent modern Christian theologians, the idea of the Kingdom of God on earth, of central significance in the teachings of Jesus and of the early Christians, has either been eliminated or "spiritualized" in Christian thought, i.e., transformed into the promise of individual post-mortem reward in Heaven. Schmemann attributes the loss of eschatological

9 Georges Florovsky, *Creation and Redemption* (Belmont, Massachusetts: Nordland Publishing Company, 1976), p. 16.
10 Father Alexander Schmemann, *Church, World, Mission* (Crestwood, New York: St. Vladimir's Seminary Press, 1979), p. 151.

21

consciousness in the *Orthodox* Church to its Westerniza-
tion, or "Western captivity."[11]

Orthodox philosophers and theologians have undoubtedly been more successful in preserving the idea of
the Kingdom of God than Western Christianity has been.
Yet the efforts to accommodate Herself to worldly power
over the centuries, and to the forces of secularism in the
modern world, have had an impact on Eastern as well as
Western Christianity, and it is far more likely for the modern Christian to accept the gospel of other-worldly salvation than it is to recognize the this-worldly eschatological
thrust that was characteristic of Jesus and of the Church in
its infancy.

The Kingdom of God in the New Testament

Yet the central idea of the gospel, according to the
Gospel's own testimony, is the idea of the Kingdom of God.
As Jesus stated, "I must preach the good news of the Kingdom of God to the other cities also; for I was sent for this
purpose" (Luke 4:43). The Gospel of Mark tells us that Jesus
opened his active earthly ministry in the following way:
"Now after John was arrested, Jesus came into Galilee,
preaching the gospel of God, and saying 'The time is fulfilled and the Kingdom of God is at hand; repent, and believe in the gospel' " (Mark 1:14-15). Over eighty times in
the Gospels Jesus refers to the Kingdom.[12] After Christ's
resurrection, He appeared to His followers "over a period

11 Father Alexander Schmemann, *Great Lent* (Crestwood, New
York: St. Vladimir's Seminary Press, 1974), p. 117.
12 Howard Snyder, *The Community of the King* (Downers Grove,
Illinois: InterVarsity Press, 1978), p. 14.

of forty days and spoke about the Kingdom of God" (Acts 1:3).

Christian witness testifies that the promises to Israel made by God were being fulfilled in the work and mission of Jesus. The Christ-event represented both the supernatural breaking into history of God's Kingdom in the person of Jesus—the healings, the miracles, the blessings bestowed upon those who accepted Jesus' yoke—and the then (and now) as yet future eschatological consummation of the Kingdom, the final deliverance from mortality and the reestablishment of communion between God and humanity. The mission of Jesus "brought to men an actual foretaste of the eschatological salvation"[13]—however, "the saving power of the Kingdom was not yet universally operative. It was resident in Jesus and in those whom he commissioned (Matthew 10:8)."[14] Father Georges Florovsky has termed this biblical view an "inaugurated eschatology." " 'The ultimate' (or the 'new') has already entered history, although the final stage is not yet attained....The Kingdom has been already inaugurated but not yet fulfilled."[15]

It is important that the miracles not be misinterpreted as mere symbolic imagery. The miracles, as James Kalas observes, are "the bringing of the Kingdom, the routing of the forces of evil which rule the world."[16] Jesus Himself substantiated His own messianic claim by pointing to the

13 George Eldon Ladd, *The Presence of the Future* (Grand Rapids, Michigan: Eerdmans Publishing Company, 1974), p. 217.

14 Ibid., p. 211.

15 Father Georges Florovsky, *Bible, Church, Tradition: An Eastern Orthodox View* (Belmont, Massachusetts: Nordland Publishing Company, 1972), p. 36.

16 James Kalas, *The Significance of the Synoptic Miracles*, p. 83.

miracles and healings.

> Now when John heard in prison about the deeds of Christ, he sent word by his disciples and said to Him, "Are you He who is to come or shall we look for another?" And Jesus answered them, "Go, and tell John what you see and hear; the blind receive their sight, and the lame walk, lepers are cleansed and the deaf hear, and the dead are raised up and the poor have good news preached to them." (Matthew 11:2-5)

But it was not merely because Jesus was a healer and miracle worker that He was able to arouse the most intense messianic aspirations of His followers, and to motivate them to completely transform their lives and to follow Him. It was because these miracles were viewed by Jesus, and by the early Church from within the context of Jewish eschatology—as the fulfillment of the history of promises made by God to Israel. Commenting on Jesus' announcement, "The time is fulfilled, and the Kingdom of God is at hand," Beasley Murray writes, "One must read the prophets to grasp the immense dynamic of the expectation, the unbroken and ever newly awakened faith in an 'absolute future' of God. Only then does one know what this statement says in which the faith of early Christianity has become shaped, the unsurpassable future of God has begun."[17]

Schmemann makes a similar point. The modern Christian accepts the Old Testament because he believes in the New. But the early Christians "believed in the New because they had seen, experienced, and perceived the fulfillment of the Old. Jesus was the Christ, the Messiah—the

---

17 Beasley Murray, *Jesus and the Kingdom of God,* p. 77.

one in whom all the promises and prophecies of the Old Testament were fulfilled. They experienced Christianity as the beginning of the 'Lord's Day,' toward which the whole history of the chosen people was moving. Thus Christianity was the fulfillment of the 'one sacred history of the Covenant between God and His people.' "[18]

After Jesus' death, the Crucifixion and Resurrection become the focal point in St. Paul's theology. He will have nothing of a spiritualized Christianity. He vigorously defends an inaugurated eschatology, arguing against those who would deny or minimize the universal and futurist significance of Christ's resurrection. Beker succinctly summarizes Paul's position: "The climax of the history of salvation is not the resurrection of Christ and His present glory but the impending glory of God, on behalf of whom Christ exercised His function as 'Lord' (Philippians 2:11) and as intercessor" (Romans 8:31-34).[19]

Paul admonishes those who deny that Christ's resurrection portends the final victory of humanity over death. "If I fought wild beasts in Ephesus for merely human reasons, what have I gained? If the dead are not raised, 'Let us eat and drink for tomorrow we die.' Do not be misled" (1 Corinthians 15:32-33).

Paul is emphatic: Death is not part of the Kingdom of God. "Now this I say, brethren, that flesh and blood cannot inherit the Kingdom of God; neither does corruption inherit incorruption....So when this corruptible shall have

---

18 Father Alexander Schmemann, *Introduction to Liturgical Theology* (London: The Faith Press, 1966), pp. 47-48.

19 J. Christiaan Beker, *Paul the Apostle: The Triumph of God in Life and Thought* (Philadelphia: Fortress Press, 1980), p. 363.

put on incorruption, and this mortal shall have put on immortality, then shall be brought to pass the saying that is written, 'Death shall be swallowed up in victory. O, death, where is thy sting? O, grave, where is thy victory?'" (1 Corinthians 15:50–55).

As Beker emphasizes, Paul's eschatology is radically different from the spiritualistic eschatologies that are dominant in Christianity today. "The apocalyptic vision of God's Kingdom is part and parcel of Paul's Christology, for the coming of the Messiah is the promise of God's public presence in history. Thus Paul's Christology cannot live without the parousia of Christ, and he is unable to collapse eschatology into Christology or to spiritualize the messianic hope, as Catholic Christianity did after him."[20]

The eclipse of the eschatological interpretation of the Christ-event, and of the vision of the Kingdom of God on earth, so prominent in the teachings of Jesus and St. Paul, has been disastrous for the Christian mission. It is obvious that St. Paul and the early Christians thought that the new aeon was imminent—they did not reckon on a "delay" continuing two millennia to date. I contend that, in large part, the "delay of the parousia" is a result of the loss of Christianity's eschatological thrust.[21] Prospective converts have been deprived of the strongest motive for following the way of Christ: that by so doing we will be advancing

20 Ibid., pp. 345-346.
21 The delay of the parousia is a much debated topic in theology. See, for example, Adrio König, *The Eclipse of Christ in Eschatology* (Grand Rapids, Eerdsman Publishing Company, 1989). König writes, "The imminence of His return serves as a call to vigilance, not as neutral information from which we can calculate the time of His return" (p. 198).

on the path that will lead us through the gates of Paradise.

John MacQuarrie has pointed to the "extraordinary power" that such eschatological convictions exert on the life of people who hold them. He wrote, "To believe that one was living in the face of an end that might happen tomorrow, and, in any case, very soon, must have imparted a tremendous sense of urgency, responsibility, and vitality....Such a partial explanation of the amazing energy of the early Christian community is to be sought in its intense conviction of the approaching end."[22]

Laborers with God

But there is another problem that faces those of us attempting to fan the messianic embers still glowing within the collective imagination of humanity. Many of the few who do have an eschatological perspective believe that the process of salvation is entirely dependent upon God. This belief seems to stem from the Protestant fear that acknowledging the power of human beings somehow compromises the "sovereignty" of God."[23] It is sadly ironic that Jürgen Moltmann, probably the single most prominent theologian with an eschatological interpretation of Christianity, de-

22 Cited in J. Christiaan Beker, *Paul's Apocalyptic Gospel* (Philadelphia: Fortress Press, 1982), p. 104.

23 As John Howard Yoder put it, "That God is gracious to me is the good news that Zinzendorf, Wesley, Kierkegaard, and today both Rudolf Bultmann and Billy Graham (in their very different ways) have derived from Luther and have labored to keep unclouded by any effort...to base upon it a social program or any other human work. To safeguard the pure gratuitousness of grace, any binding correlation with human goals or achievements must be studiously kept in second place." John Howard Yoder, *The Royal Priesthood*, p. 73.

nies that human beings can have any influence over the process of salvation.[24]

Orthodox theologians and philosophers have shed *new* light on the dynamics of salvation that has been obscured by the determinism of many Western Christians, for the Orthodox Church has always maintained that salvation is a divine-human process. Contrary to Moltmann's assertion, the following comment by Martin Buber is very much in the spirit of Christianity as well as Judaism: "The redemption of the world is left to the power of our conversion. God has no wish for any other means of perfecting His creation than by our help. He will not reveal His Kingdom until we have laid its foundations."[25]

The 20th century Orthodox theologian Vladimir Lossky has eloquently described the Orthodox perspective on the necessity of human cooperation in the process of salvation. This view is in accord with Jesus, who exhorts us to "seek" the Kingdom of God, and of St. Paul who described Christians as "laborers together with God" (1 Corinthians 3:9). Lossky writes:

> Personal beings constitute the peak of creation, since they can become God by free choice and grace....The person is the highest creation of God only because God gives it the possibility of love, therefore of refusal. God risks the eternal ruin of His highest creation, precisely that it may be the highest....

24 See Jürgen Moltmann, *Theology of Hope* (Minneapolis: Fortress Press, 1993), pp. 122-124. Does Moltmann think that human beings can continue to slaughter each other, despoil the planet, and ignore Christ's commandments and still God's Kingdom will dawn on earth?

25 Cited in Ibid., p. 124.

Certainly man was created by the will of God alone; but He cannot be deified by it alone. A single will for creation, but two for deification. A single will to raise up the image, but two to make the image into a likeness. The love of God for man is so great that it cannot constrain; for there is no love without respect.[26]

Probably the most masterly exposition after St. Paul of the dialectic between man and God and of the cosmic and social dimensions of salvation was written by St. Maximus the Confessor in the 7th century.[27] Vladimir Lossky wrote that St. Maximus "has described with an incomparable power and fullness the mission devolving upon man."[28] According to St. Maximus, man is given the divine task of leading the multiplicity and duality of the universe to a final union. This task was presented to human beings in the beginning, but its realization was interrupted by the Fall and required the incarnation of Christ, who acted as a model for all human beings.[29] As Meyendorff puts it, "God not only grants beings their existence, and in the case of man, an eternal existence; but He also assigns to them a goal to reach, and in the case of

26   Vladimir Lossky, *Orthodox Theology; An Introduction* (Crestwood, New York: St. Vladimir's Seminary Press, 1989), pp. 72-73.

27   Maximus was brutally martyred by some people within the Church in 664 for espousing a "heresy" that became official Church doctrine a few years after his death.

28   Vladimir Lossky, *Orthodox Theology* (Crestwood, New York, St. Vladimir's Seminary Press, 1989), p. 74.

29   Lars Thunberg, *Man and the Cosmos: The Vision of St. Maximus, The Confessor* (Crestwood, New York: St. Vladimir's Seminary Press, 1985).

man this goal implies a free movement toward God."[30] Maximus denotes five fundamental dualities that must be unified: the created and the uncreated, the intelligible and the tangible, heaven and earth, paradise and the universe, and male and female. Although we are assisted by divine grace, our salvation, that is, our reintegration into the natural state "depends on our will," as Maximus put it.[31]

The Russian Eschatological Renaissance

Eschatological expectations reached a peak in Russia at the end of the 19th century and the beginning of the 20th century. Nikolai Berdyaev, one of the most remarkable of Russian Orthodox philosophers who embraced the eschatological interpretation of Christianity, believed that the Russian people were eschatological in nature, they are "a people of the End."[32] Berdyaev wrote, "The whole of primitive Christianity was eschatological. It expected the second Advent of Christ and the coming of the Kingdom of God."[33] He believed that historical Christianity failed in the sense that the Kingdom of God had not come. This failure was a result of the accommodation of Christian revelation to the "kingdom of this world."[34] Consequently, the messianic expectations had been driven inward, and later on made their appearance in a secularized form.[35]

30 John Meyendorff, *Christ in Eastern Christian Thought* (Crestwood, New York: St. Vladimir's Seminary Press, 1975), p. 37.

31 Cited in Ibid., p. 149.

32 Nikolai Berdyaev, *The Russian Idea* (New York: Lindisfarne Press, 1992), p. 208.

33 Ibid., p. 210.

34 Ibid., p. 210.

35 Nikolai Berdyaev, *The Divine and the Human* (London: G Bles, 1949), p. 173.

This, of course, explains the assumption of power by the Bolsheviks, who strongly appealed to the messianic aspirations of the Russian people.

Berdyaev was critical of what he termed the "official ecclesiasticism" of the Orthodox Church, but his sharpest criticisms were directed against Western Christianity, particularly Protestantism. In traditional theology, "human life has been regarded as a penal process which God has set on foot against man the criminal. The penal interpretation of redemption...has penetrated deeply into Christianity."[36] Berdyaev called for a break with all legalistic ways of understanding Christianity and of all interpretations of Christianity as a religion of individual salvation.[37] "The Kingdom of God," he wrote, "is the transfiguration of the world, not only the transfiguration of the individual man, but also the transfiguration of the social and the cosmic, and that is the end of this world, of the world of wrong and ugliness, and it is the principle of a new world, a world of right and beauty."[38]

The realization of the Kingdom of God in this sense of the term (not merely as individual salvation) requires not merely ascetic discipline but the utilization of all the creative powers of man. Berdyaev stated that "everything great in human creative effort enters into the Kingdom of God."[39] He wrote, "The end of the world is a divine–human enterprise....The creative act of man is needed for the coming of the Kingdom of God. God is in need of and

36   Nikolai Berdyaev, *Truth and Revelation* (London: G Bles, 1953), p. 113.

37   Ibid., p. 125.

38   Nikolai Berdyaev, *The Russian Idea* (New York: Lindisfarne Press, 1992), p. 210.

39   Nikolai Berdyaev, *Truth and Revelation*, p. 125.

awaits it."[40] Or, as he observed elsewhere, "When man does that to which he is called, then only will the second coming of Christ take place, and then there will be a new heaven and a new earth."[41]

Berdyaev hailed Vladimir Solovyov (1853-1900) as the most distinguished representative of Russian religious philosophy in the 19th century. Alexander Schmemann called him simply "the most important Russian philosopher."[42] Schmemann believed that he helped free Orthodox thought from its "Western captivity," i.e., from "the internal Latinization of Orthodox theology, from which it has not freed itself completely even now."[43] Berdyaev also saw Solovyov as the prophet of a Christian renaissance that would lead eventually not to individual salvation but to the realization of the Kingdom of God on earth.[44]

Solovyov believed that human history was divided into two periods. The first half prepared the environment for the birth of Christ, the God-man. The second half after Christ prepares the environment for the revelation of the Kingdom of God, for "the perfect moral order realized by a new humanity which spiritually grows out of the God-man."[45]

40 Nikolai Berdyaev, *The Beginning and the End* (London: G Bles, 1952), p. 251.

41 Nikolai Berdyaev, *Slavery and Freedom* (New York: Harper and Row, 1939), p. 268.

42 Father Alexander Schmemann, *Ultimate Questions: Anthology of Modern Russian Religious Thought* (Crestwood, New York: St. Vladimir's Seminary Press, 1977).

43 Ibid., p. 8.

44 Nikolai Berdyaev, *The Russian Idea* (New York: Lindisfarne Press, 1992), p. 188.

45 Vladimir Solovyov, *The Justification of the Good: An Essay in Moral Philosophy* (New York: McMillan, 1918), p. 193.

Solovyov believed that the Kingdom of God had to grow gradually within the old order if it would eventually manifest itself. This process is both organic and voluntary. He observed that the "Kingdom preached by Christ is something that moves, approaches, comes. It has different aspects. It is within us, and yet it is manifested outwardly; it grows in mankind and in the whole world through a certain subjective organic process, and it is also taken by free effort of our will."[46] If Solovyov is correct, then the sins of historic Christianity are both tragic by-products of its immaturity and acts for which the Christian community bears responsibility.

Solovyov rejected the Western idea that man must play a "merely passive part in the divine work" as a "crude counterfeit of Christianity....For appearance's sake the view is supported by the argument that God is everything and man is nothing, but in truth this false humility is rebellion against God." For God magnified humanity in Christ and gave them the power to become "sons of God." Solovyov continues, "Sons of the kingdom of freedom are called to conscious and independent cooperation in the work of the Father."[47]

Needless to say, Solovyov does not disparage the significance of God's work in Christ. But we do not do justice to Christianity by reducing it to an abstract *ism*, to a credo. Rather, we must morally transform ourselves in accord with the spirit of Christ. At the same time the individual's moral achievement, "if it is to obtain completion, must

46 Vladimir Solovyov, "The Essence of Christianity" in *A Solovyov Anthology*, ed. S.L. Frank (New York: Charles Scribner's Sons, 1950), p. 44.
47 Ibid., pp. 47-48.

inevitably enter into the social movement of all humanity and form part...of the general divinely-human process of universal history." The person who succeeds in doing this "finds the Kingdom of God not in himself only, but also in the objective course and structure of the Revelation, in the actual manifestations of the Deity in past and present humanity, and in the ideal anticipation of other, more perfect manifestations in the future."[48] There is something destined in all of this, "yet individual freedom is preserved, for everyone is free to use or not to use for himself the universal religious heritage of mankind, to enter or not to enter with his own living powers into the organic development of the Kingdom of God."[49]

Solovyov believed that the foundations of the Kingdom of God were political and social as well as spiritual. He argued that in order to realize Christian principles in the collective life of mankind, we must be concerned "not with preserving and strengthening at all costs the existing social forms and groups in secular Christianity, but with regenerating and transforming them in the Christian spirit."[50]

Solovyov tended to rely on organic metaphors that do not do full justice to the personal nature of man's relationship to God, and to the role of God the Father in the process of salvation. Nevertheless, he illuminates many aspects of Christian missionary work that have been obscured by the loss of eschatological consciousness in Western Christianity.

Solovyov's vision of the Kingdom of God on earth is

48 Ibid., p. 45.
49 Ibid., pp. 45-46.
50 Ibid., p. 49.

profound and numinous: The Kingdom of God is the restoration of the unity of all creation and the harmony of all beings. It is the accomplishment of the interpenetration of the divine and the human principles—this will be the conquest of human mortality: the attainment of eternal life. This unity is not immediate, as before the Fall. It will not be characterized by pristine innocence, as it is the result of a free act, "of a double exploit, that of divine and human self-renunciation because, for the true unification of the two principles, the free participation and action of both are necessary.[51]

Berdyaev described Solovyov's vision of the Kingdom of God as "the all-embracing unity of the world, the divine cosmos, in which there is no separation of the parts from the whole, no enmity or discord, in which there is nothing abstract and self-assertive. It was a vision of beauty."[52] It is the product Berdyaev asserted of both "an intellectual and an erotic intuition."[53]

The Recovery of Eschatology

The Christian diagnosis of the human situation after the Fall is that all creation is divided, the universe is reigned by the principle of division. Schmemann wrote, "The essence of the fallen world is that division, the separation of each from all, reigns in it. This is not overcome by the 'natural' love of certain people for certain others, and it triumphs

51 Vladimir Solovyov, *Divine Humanity* (Hudson, New York: Lindesfarne Press, 1995), p. 159.

52 Nikolai Berdyaev, *The Russian Idea* (New York: Lindisfarne Press, 1992), p. 183.

53 Ibid., p. 183.

and is fulfilled in the ultimate 'separation'—death."[54] We live in a society based on the principle of division —where groups and individuals seek to advance their interests by limiting or destroying the life opportunities of other groups and individuals. It is a society based on existential—and literal—cannibalism, to borrow Thomas Szasz' term,[55] where fortunes can be made and high status achieved by destroying the lives of other human beings. (Look at Freud!)[56]

St. Paul viewed the Church as the paradigm of unity. He used a variety of metaphors to convey a sense of this unity, which is firstly a unity of God and man, Christ and humanity. The Church is the Body of Christ, and Christ is the Head of the Church. When Christians contended for primacy within the Church, St. Paul reminded each one to be content with the gifts and the graces he had received, just as in the body each member is satisfied with its position and performs its duties for the benefit of all. (See, for example, Romans 12:3-8.) The Church thus becomes a "city on the hill" (Matthew 5:11), providing an example for society to emulate.[57]

54 Alexander Schmemann, *The Eucharist* (Crestwood, New York: St. Vladimir's Seminary Press, 1988), p. 137.

55 See Thomas Szasz' foreword inSeth Farber, *Madness, Heresy and the Rumor of Angels: A Revolt Against the Mental Health System* (Chicago, Open Court Press, 1993) p xv.

56 See chapters 5 and 6.

57 The Indian philosopher Sri Auribindo wrote that if society were based on the principle of spiritual unity, there would be no conflict between order and liberty because "free individuals enamored of unity would be compelled by themselves, by their own need, to accommodate perfectly their own growth with the growth of their fellows and would not feel themselves complete except in the free growth of others." Thus law would become "the child of freedom."

The Church has to exhibit "the new mode of life," that of the "world to come."[58] Florovsky wrote, "The sacred history of redemption is now the history of the Church; that is, the Body of God."[59] Unity must come from above, not from below, to be effective. "The center of unity is the Lord and the power that effects and enacts the unity is the Spirit."[60]

Schmemann has demonstrated masterfully that "unity from above" is experienced in (ideally) and effected through the liturgy, particularly the Eucharist. He has decried the disconnection between sacraments and eschatology that took place in the West, but also to a lesser degree in the East ("the Western captivity"). Gradually the understanding of the sacraments was transformed from the modality for the fulfillment of the Church as eschatological community into mere means of individual sanctification.[61]

The eternal "wonder" of the worship of Christ is that "it transforms the stranger (and each stranger in his depths is an enemy) into a brother."[62] The communion with God and with his "brothers in Christ" that the Christian experiences (hopefully) in the liturgy is "unity from 'above'

Sri Aurobindo, *Social and Political Thought* (Pondicherry, India: Sri Aurobindo Ashram, 1985).

58 Father Georges Florovsky, *Bible, Church, Tradition: An Eastern Orthodox View* (Belmont, Massachusetts: Nordland Publishing Company, 1972), p. 69.

59 Ibid., p. 36.

60 Ibid., p. 61.

61 Alexander Schmemann, *Church, World, Mission* (Crestwood, New York: St. Vladimir's Seminary Press, 1988), p. 157.

62 Alexander Schmemann, *The Eucharist* (Crestwood, New York: St. Vladimir's Seminary Press, 1988), p. 139.

and imparts to him a deep sense of 'peace and joy' in the Holy Spirit."[63] In other words, through the Church, in the liturgy, the Christian receives a foretaste of the eschatological salvation, just as the first Christians did in the presence of Jesus.[64]

This has (insofar as it occurs!) two significant consequences. On the one hand, "through contrast with the beauty and wonder of creation [revealed in worship]...the darkness and failure of the world is discovered."[65] Precisely because the Church experiences the divine unity of creation, she is separated, estranged from "this world," which she knows now is the "fallen world" captivated by death.[66]

On the other hand, the experience of unity from above, and the consequent estrangement from this world, gives birth to the fervent desire to reunify the fallen, divided world. This is the eschatological spirit that imparts impetus to the Christian mission, to give "unchanging and radiant testimony to the reality of the Kingdom of God."[67] And it also undergirds, I would add, the effort to oppose

63 Alexander Schmemann, *Church, World, Mission* (Crestwood, New York: St. Vladimir's Seminary Press, 1988), p. 152.

64 But, according to Schmemann, this transformation of consciousness rarely occurs in the liturgy, precisely because Christians do not understand this is the true purpose of the liturgy. Instead they approach it as an "aesthetic experience" or a "therapeutic exercise." Alexander Schmemann, *Liturgy and Tradition* (Crestwood, New York: St. Vladimir's Seminary Press, 1990), p. 100.

65 Alexander Schmemann, *For the Life of the World* (Crestwood, New York: St. Vladimir's Seminary Press, 1988), p. 61.

66 Alexander Schmemann, *The Eucharist* (Crestwood, New York: St. Vladimir's Seminary Press, 1988), p. 152.

67 Alexander Schmemann, *Church, World, Mission* (Crestwood, New York: St. Vladimir's Seminary Press, 1979), p. 156.

exploitation, and to transform the secular world and its institutions in accord with the spirit of Christ.

In this book I have focused on only several particular tasks before us, albeit of colossal scope: working to bring about the demise of the human service professions, replacing the mental health system with associations based on Christian principles of care, and transcending the Augustinian and secularist worldview that has imprisoned humanity in a culture of gloom and/or nihilism for centuries. The accomplishment of these tasks constitutes a major step toward unifying the polarities of a divided world and creating the conditions necessary for the consummation of the process of salvation.

I call upon my Orthodox brethren to lead the way, and to set an example for other Christians by entirely repudiating modern Psychology/Psychiatry, as well as Augustinian and secular strains of Christianity, and by immediately beginning to address our missionary work to, and seeking to incorporate into the Church, those individuals who are undergoing spiritual crises, and are thus most in danger of being stigmatized as "mentally ill" and destroyed by the "mental health system."

I submit that we will not have the courage to make these changes, or the strength to acknowledge—let alone resolve—the problems that threaten the very existence of the human species unless we recover the eschatological spirit of the early Church. I have surveyed in this chapter the eschatologies not only of Jesus, St. Paul, and the early Church, but also of several more contemporary thinkers. Because these philosophers were, I believe, inspired by the Holy Spirit and because their style of expression may appear more familiar (due to their cultural and temporal proximity to us), it is likely that they may help convince some of my readers that eschatology is not an anachronistic superstition that modern man has outgrown but the very substance of Christian faith.

It is our task as Christians, and as Orthodox, to rouse the messianic aspirations that lie dormant in the collective imagination of humanity, to rekindle the conviction that salvation is possible, to encourage the determination to break with the habits of the past, and to do everything within human power to foster the realization of God's Kingdom on earth.

PART ONE

CHAPTER 1

The Reign of Augustine

There is more worth in all the vermin in the world than in man, for he is a creature where the image of God has been effaced and where the good where God has put in it has been corrupted. There is nothing in him but sin....
                    John Calvin[68]

Society and culture has been shaped for centuries by a deep-structure of philosophical assumptions that have prevented the realization of humanity's spiritual potential, leading ultimately to the debacle of modern civilization. I believe that this deep-structure was the creation of Augustine (in *The City of God*), and of his followers Luther and Calvin.

There are six distinctive premises (or consequences) of Augustinianism, all of which one finds in covert secularized form in modern Freudian theory, thus illustrating

68 Cited in David Cairns, *The Image of God in Man*, (London: SCM Press, 1953) p. 139.

This is an idiom foreign to modern ears, and it strikes us more as an insult than it does as a theological statement. But if the same kind of sentiment is expressed today in "scientific/psychological" language, its evaluative components are thereby disguised, and we are likely to accept it as a fact about a person or a group of persons, rather than an attitude towards them. Only a few advanced thinkers have recognized the demeaning nature of the kind of language we use to describe those individuals whom psychiatry deems "the mentally ill."

that although two worldviews may appear very different—even antithetical—they have the same deep-structure that is the true determinant of their impact upon humanity, nature, and culture.

The core premise of Augustinianism—that which defines its essence and has had the most pervasive and enduring influence upon Western Christianity is that there is a divide between God and humanity, between God and nature, which cannot be removed or bridged.

This premise is a self-fulfilling prophecy that militates against any efforts on our part to restore communion with God, to recognize His presence in the universe, and to worship and adore Him both in His transcendent being and in and through the world He has created.

God has been relegated to the heavens, and we no longer regard nature as the sacred epiphany of God but as mere matter to be quantified and exploited for our materialistic and frequently destructive goals. Suffice it to state that the idea that the human being is created in the image of God, and thus ought properly to be treated with reverence, and with self-reverence, i.e., holiness, has been all but banished from modern life.

Christ's Ontology of Plenitude[69]

Every act of perceiving or interpreting the world is structured by an implicit or explicit worldview. This is to

69   The Christian ontology of John Milbank (see *Theology and Social Theory: Beyond Secular Reason* [Oxford, UK: Blackwell, 1995], which he eloquently describes as "the ontological priority of peace over conflict" (p. 390) is congruent with my own "ontology of plenitude," and he decisively breaks from what I have termed an "ontology of deficiency and flaw." Yet remarkably enough, Milbank describes his

say the world we inhabit is not independent of our philosophical assumptions about the world but is in significant measure a product of these beliefs. The most fundamental dimension of a worldview is ontological: the theory about the nature of being, of reality, of existence. The ontological dimension generates, or at least coheres with, an anthropological and a theological dimension.

There are essentially two types of ontologies: On the one hand there is a pessimistic ontology of flaw, of deficiency, of absence, and on the other hand there is an optimistic ontology of wholeness, of plenitude, of presence. One might say that the former posits a deficiency, whereas the latter apprehends a plenitude in the depths of the heart of being. This characteristic is what being (call it reality or existence, if you prefer) essentially is. It is its distinguishing feature, how it is experienced.

Modern secular theories (if they are consistent) are

ontology as quasi-Augustinian, and I describe mine as anti-Augustinian. How is this possible?

Because Milbank, like so many other scholars and theologians, ignores what is most offensive in the elder Augustine's book *The City of God*. Although Milbank critiques Augustine for sanctioning the use of violence against heretics, he claims that this policy is inconsistent with Augustine's ontology of peace. Milbank states that the "ontological priority of peace over conflict" is the principle "undergirding Augustine's critique of Plato." Milbank tells us that for Plato and Aristotle goodness and happiness occupy "certain privileged sites of self-presence over against an irredeemably chaotic and conflictual cosmos" (p. 262). To be more specific, peace and happiness exist only for the privileged classes and only "within the city walls" (p. 392). For Augustine, Milbank claims, peace is "co-terminous with all Being whatsoever" (p. 392).

This is an astonishing misreading of *The City of God* that is typical of many Christians who simply will not come to terms with ineluctably ontologies of flaw insofar as they are based on Darwinian or neo-Darwinian biological paradigms. Even in its more optimistic, non-reductionistic form this model inevitably posits the subordination of the individual to the species: the species develops at the expense of the individual, who is trampled under foot in the forward march of evolving Nature.

Eastern cultures tend to be religious and based on more optimistic ontologies. Classical Hinduism is an ontology of plenitude. It maintains that the true features of human existence are consciousness and bliss; it is only ignorance that prevents this realization. Seekers (and in the Hindu anthropology all human beings are essentially religious seekers) discover at the conclusion of their quest that in the depths of their soul they are holy and in their nature identical to God. The doctrine of reincarnation relativizes the meaning of an individual's suffering because the individual is destined after the course of many incarnations to

Augustine's limitations. Augustine's ontology is remarkably similar to Plato. Here, too, peace and happiness exist only for privileged classes—Augustine's elect—and only within a certain privileged site: the City of God. In the very book and chapter of *The City of God* that Milbank claims exemplifies Augustine's commitment to peace and charity as the highest virtues (p. 411), Augustine states, "On the other hand, the doom in store for those who are not of the City of God is an unending wretchedness...." (See Vernon Bourke, *The City of God* [New York: Doubleday, 1948], pp. 481-482.) Augustine goes on to emphasize this point by stating that what will make the torment of those predestined to "hell" intolerable is its "permanence," "since the punishment must never end" (p. 482). Although Milbank states that Augustine considers forgiveness the supreme virtue, the God that Augustine worships will not or cannot forgive all human beings, as He consigns some to eternal punishment, independent of their willingness or refusal to accept His grace.

transcend worldly suffering and to be reabsorbed, as it were, into God.

In Hindu philosophy, at least in its dominant form, the world is ultimately unreal; it is a dream, an illusion. It is the realization of its illusory nature that severs the ties that bind the soul of the seeker to earthly existence, characterized inexorably by suffering and death, and that enable him to embrace the reality of the formless Godhead. As in Plato's theory, knowledge brings liberation from the world of shadows.

The ontology implied by the Old and New Testaments differs from that of Hinduism. What Plato and Hinduism dismiss as the world of illusion, Jews and Christians see as our natural home. The human being is a hybrid, a natural-spiritual being, the steward of creation, the mediator between Heaven and earth.

The Jesus of the Gospels does not elaborate an ontology. Nonetheless, it is implicit in all His deeds and in the proclamation that resounds throughout the Gospel: The Kingdom of God is at hand. The glad tidings, the Good News, is that the gift of salvation is offered to all—not only to the righteous, but to sinners, to the "scum" of society. Jesus does not explain why suffering exists in God's universe—He merely announces the beginning of its end. Jesus tells His disciples, "Go back and report to John what you hear and see: The blind receives sight, the lame walk, those who have leprosy are cured, the deaf hear, the dead are raised, and the Good News is preached to the poor" (Matthew 11:4-6).

"And being asked by the Pharisees, when the Kingdom of God cometh, He answered them and said, 'The Kingdom of God cometh not with observation.... Neither shall they say, Lo, here! or, There! for lo, the Kingdom of God is in your midst'" (Luke 17:20-21). Thus Jesus proclaims an ontology of plenitude which is experienced in His presence—in His miracles, His deeds and His words— as God's infinite love and redemptive power.

God's great gift is offered through Christ. Rudolf Otto put it well, "The thing of which the parables themselves were meant to treat is the Kingdom neither as a constraining power, nor as a claim to sovereignty...but as the blessing of salvation, the blessing pure and simple, and purely and simply a blessing. A blessing does not demand, it does not work through command on the will, but by the fact that just because it is a blessing, i.e., something desired and most highly desirable, it awakens the strongest interest and thereby arouses search and exertion and surrender of everything....It is a gift which, when its meaning and value are recognized, draws human will and effort to itself."[70] Christ's anthropology depicts human beings as essentially children of God who are called upon to accept God's gift in humility.

The Reign of Augustine

The worldview and ontology that has dominated the consciousness of Western civilizations since the 4th century A.D. has been based on the thought of St. Augustine. Jaroslav Pelikan writes: "In Augustine of Hippo Western Christianity found its most influential spokesman...and there is probably no Christian theologian—Eastern or Western, ancient or medieval or modern, heretical or orthodox—

---

70 Rudolf Otto, *The Kingdom of God and the Son of Man* (London: Lutterworth Press, 1938), pp. 128–129.

whose historical influence can match his."[71] More foreboding, but more to the point of our study, Elaine Pagels writes, "From the 5th century on, Augustine's pessimistic views of sexuality, politics, and human nature would become the dominant influence on Western Christianity, both Catholic and Protestant, and color all Western culture, Christian or not, ever since."[72]

The Eastern (Greek Orthodox) Christian philosopher Phillip Sherrard (1920-1993) commented that it was remarkable and paradoxical that the same man, Augustine, the mystic and author of *Confessions*, "the man who affirmed so strongly the presence of God in the depths of his own self," was later as a doctrinal theologian responsible "more than any other Christian writer for 'consecrating' within the Christian world 'the idea of man's slavery and impotence due to original sin.'"[73] It was the later Augustine who exercised the formative influence on Christianity, thus obscuring much of the essential meaning of the Christian revelation. "It has been St. Augustine's theology which in the West has veiled down to the present day the full radiance of the Christian revelation of divine sonship—the full revelation of who man essentially is."[74]

Augustine and Original Sin

Augustine's narrative of original sin provides the medium for his understanding of being, humanity, and God.

71 Jaroslav Pelikan, *The Emergence of the Catholic Tradition* (Chicago: University of Chicago Press, 1971), p. 292.

72 Elaine Pagels, *Adam, Eve and the Serpent* (New York: Random House, 1988), p. 150.

73 Philip Sherrard, *The Eclipse of Man and Nature* (West Stockbridge, Massachusetts: Lindisfarne Press, 1987), p. 21.

74 Ibid., p. 21.

In the beginning God created Adam and Eve, and they lived in a paradise of perpetual joy. They ate of the fruits of the tree of life and became immortal. As Augustine put it, "Adam lived in paradise as he wanted to, and for as long as he wanted what God had commanded. He lived enjoying God, from whom, the Good, he also was good; and he lived without lacking anything, having it in his power to live this way forever."[75] Man had been given "a soul so endowed with reason and intelligence that it ranks man higher than all the other creatures of the earth, the sea, the air, because they lack intelligence."[76]

Etienne Gilson, paraphrasing Augustine's thoughts on Adam before the Fall, wrote, "Besides his state of perfect peace (perfect health of body, perfect peace of soul) the mind of the first man was blessed with clear light....He possessed extensive knowledge and spontaneously avoided error."[77] He was created in a state of rectitude, "possessing complete subordination of body to soul."[78] N.P. Williams states that according to Augustine's theory Adam spontaneously had a determination toward virtue that the greatest saints have acquired only through a lifetime of struggle. Augustine's idealized picture, Williams points out, goes far beyond the language of the scriptural text and beyond that conception of man's first condition of amoral infancy which appears in the

75 Cited in Jaroslav Pelikan, *The Emergence of the Catholic Tradition, Volume One,* p. 298.

76 Vernon Bourke, ed., St. Augustine, *The City of God* (New York: Doubleday, 1958), p. 263.

77 Etienne Gilson, *Introduction to the Study of Augustine,* p. 149.

78 Ibid., p. 149.

early Greek fathers.[79]

For Augustine, the grace of God enabled Adam to obey God's will, though he did not receive the irrestible grace that the elect, i.e., redeemed sinners, have today: he retained the power to choose between good and evil. But then Adam and Eve disobeyed the commandment of God and ate the forbidden fruit from the tree of good and evil. This was a deliberate defiance of God by a soul that "had taken perverse delight in its own liberty and disdained the service of God."[80] This was, as Williams paraphrases Augustine, "due to pure senseless perversity; it was a sin solely of the will and not of the appetite, and was committed, not as a result of weakness or frailty, but against a settled habit of virtue....It was an infinitely malicious self-determination of Adam's free will in hostility to and contempt of his maker."[81]

As a result of Adam's sin God withdrew his grace and deserted Adam's soul. Augustine describes this as the "death of the soul," by which he means the desertion of the soul by God and the deprivation of divine grace.[82] Banished from paradise, Adam was afflicted with God's curse: subjugation to sin, disease, and physical mortality.

Augustine asserts that all human beings bear the guilt for Adam's original sin. Without any scriptural basis other than a mistranslation of Romans 5:12, Augustine insisted that "all men are understood to have sinned in that first

79 N.P. Williams, *The Ideas of the Fall and of Original Sin* (London: Longman's Green and Company, 1927), p. 361.
80 Vernon Bourke, ed., St. Augustine, *The City of God*, p. 278.
81 N.P. Williams, *The Ideas of the Fall and of Original Sin*, p. 364.
82 Vernon Bourke, *City of God*, p. 279.

man, because all men were in him when he sinned."[83] Thus, according to Augustine, due to Adam's sin every person belongs to a "mass of perdition, to a massa damnatta," to a "unity of negativity," as Paul Tillich put it.[84] Augustine wrote, "The damned lump of humanity was lying prostrate. Nay, was wallowing in evil, was falling headlong from one wickedness to another, and joined to the faction of the angels who had sinned, it was paying the most righteous penalty of its impious treason."[85]

Baptism was necessary to acquit human beings of their crime. Thus Augustine argued that infants who did not receive baptism would be condemned to suffer the torments of eternal punishment in hell. He wrote that no one who is to be born of Adam and Eve was "less a sinner than they were. Such was the greatness of the guilt that the punishment so impaired human nature that what was originally a penal condition for the first parents who sinned became a natural consequence in all of their descendants."[86]

Not only do human beings bear the legal liability for Adam's sin, but they also suffer from it as a kind of inherited disease transmitted by Adam. The semen itself, Augustine argued, "already shackled by the bond of death," transmits the damage incurred by sin. "Everyone arising as he does from a condemned stock, is from the first necessarily evil and carnal through Adam."[87] Because it was

83 Cited in Jaroslav Pelikan, *The Emergence of the Catholic Tradition, Volume One*, p. 299.

84 Paul Tillich, *A History of Christian Thought* (New York: Harper and Row, 1968), p. 128.

85 Cited in N.P. Williams, *The Ideas of the Fall and of Original Sin.*

86 Ibid., p. 277, emphasis added.

87 Elaine Pagels, *Adam, Eve and the Serpent*, p. 114.

transmitted by natural propagation, "original sin was as universal and inevitable as life itself."[88] Thus Augustine writes, "The infant is bad: though little, he is already a great sinner."[89]

In Augustine's view, human beings thus suffer from original sin in a two-fold sense: First, they suffer from a hereditary moral disease first acquired by Adam and since then transmitted to posterity. The product of this is an unbridled concupiscence that is not subject to human control, even by "the most godly and righteous."[90] Although Augustine does not deny the freedom of the will in theory, he states, "In point of fact it always freely chooses evil under the overwhelming influence of concupiscence, or of the devil's power."[91]

Second, and more importantly, human beings suffer from original sin in the sense of guilt—of an inherited legal liability to judicial punishment for Adam's sin, for the sin of humanity in Adam. It is the guilt that human beings have incurred as a result of that sin. It is this legal guilt that is removed immediately by the act of baptism, and it is for this reason that infants who die without baptism, according to Augustine, must suffer eternal punishment in hell.

The sin of Adam—and of humanity through him—was such a grievous offense against God's justice that all

88 As Jaroslav Pelikan paraphrases Augustine, *The Emergence of the Catholic Tradition*, p. 300.

89 Cited in Jean Delumeau, *Sin and Fear; The Emergence of a Western Guilt Culture, 13th-18th Centuries* (New York: St. Martin's Press, 1990), p. 269.

90 Cited in Elaine Pagels, *Adam, Eve and the Serpent*, p. 113.

91 Cited in N.P. Williams, *The Ideas of the Fall and of Original Sin*, p. 368.

human beings deserve to suffer eternal punishment. But because of God's infinite mercy, a small predestined elect will be saved. Through no merit of their own, by the sacrament of baptism they will be acquitted of the crime of original sin and spared the eternal pains of hell. Although the sickness of original sin will remain (manifesting itself in concupiscence), the infusion of God's grace through the sacraments of the Church will gradually work to heal the infection and give the redeemed the power to persevere in good works, finally cleansing them of the taint of original sin after they die.

Augustine repeats again and again that all human beings deserve to suffer eternally. He writes in *The City of God*, "Of course, once the whole mass of mankind was, as it were, cankered in its roots, there was no question of men meriting a place in His City.... [N]o one can help but acknowledge how gratuitous and undeserved is the grace which delivers him when he sees so clearly the contrast between his privileged, personal immunity and the fate of the penalized community whose punishment he was justly condemned to share."[92]

Unlike Augustine, a number of Christians did not accept the idea that the God of Christ did not favor the salvation of all. Why would a loving God predestine the salvation of just a small percentage of humanity? Augustine answered this in *The City of God*. He states that God wished to demonstrate both "the power of merciful grace," as well as "the might of just retribution." He explained, "If all had remained condemned to the punishment entailed by just condemnation, then God's merciful grace would not have been seen at work in anyone; on the other hand, if all had

92 Vernon Bourke, ed., St. Augustine, *The City of God*, p. 319.

been transferred from darkness into light, the truth of God's vengeance would not have been made evident. Now there are many more condemned by vengeance than are released by mercy; and the reason for this is that it should in this way be made plain what was the due of all mankind."[93]

Some of Augustine's opponents charged him with being unbiblical and cited 1 Timothy 2:4, where it is stated that God "wants all men to be saved and to come to a knowledge of the truth." Augustine responded that "all men" meant all the predestined, because every kind of human being was represented among them.

To those who objected to the injustice that God would arbitrarily predestine one group for salvation and another group for damnation while both were equal in worth (or rather worthlessness), Augustine responded that the will of God is "inscrutable" and not subject to the comprehension of human beings. Divine justice is so much loftier than human justice that we must not doubt Him to be just "even when He does what seems to men unjust, or what, if done by a man, would actually be unjust."[94]

In fairness, Augustine did not view creation as entirely despoiled by the Fall, nor did he espouse a doctrine of human nature as utterly ruined, or totally depraved. He explicitly states, "That light of reason which makes man an image of God has not been extinguished altogether."[95] He eloquently praises the talents of human beings that reflect the power and generosity of God: "There have been discovered and perfected, by the natural genius of man,

93 Jean Delumeau, *Sin and Fear; The Emergence of a Western Guilt Culture, 13th-18th Centuries*, p. 285.
94 Cited in Williams, p. 381.
95 Vernon Bourke, ed., St. Augustine, *The City of God*, p. 525.

innumerable arts and skills which minister not only to the necessities of life but also to human enjoyment."[96] Furthermore, "the completeness of scientific knowledge is beyond all words and becomes all the more astonishing when one pursues any single aspect of this immense corpus of information."[97] All of these traits constitute what Augustine terms "this noble human nature,"[98] which remains despite the "death" of the soul by the Fall.

Even the fallen world reflects God's glory. "What words can describe the myriad beauties of land and sea and sky? Just think of the illimitable abundance in the marvelous loveliness of light, or of the beauty of the sun and moon and stars, of shadowy glades in the woods and of the colors and perfume of flowers, of the songs and plumage of so many varieties of birds, of the innumerable animals of every species...."[99]

At times Augustine is so effusive in his description of the manifestations of human nobility one wonders if he is not ambivalent about his assertion that human beings deserve to suffer eternal torment. Yet the skills and talents that human beings possess do not mitigate their guilt. To the contrary, by pointing to the generosity of God they demonstrate the blessed life human beings would have led if they had not fallen. Thus the noble traits highlight human beings' guilt, their responsibility for what Augustine terms "an enormous iniquity."[100]

96 Ibid., p. 526.
97 Ibid., p. 527.
98 Ibid., p. 527.
99 Ibid., p. 529.
100 Ibid., p. 527.

CHAPTER 2

The Augustine Revision

Augustine's theology implies that finally it is not really God who rules but evil. It is Evil Man—Adam—who destroys the original plenitude and the all-sufficiency of being. Now that paradise has been lost, it can never be recovered. Being is deficient. While before the Fall humanity lived in organic unity under the benevolent guardianship of God, it is now split eternally into two segments: a large majority destined to permanent estrangement from God and eternal torment in hell, and a small segment destined to be reunited with God in heaven. Yet despite their different destinies all currently belong to a "mass of perdition." This is why Paul Tillich, an Augustinian, wrote with some exaggeration (considering the respective destiny of the two groups), "This is the most powerful emphasis on the solidarity of mankind in the tragedy of sin."[101]

Tillich might have stated also that God Himself in implicated in solidarity with mankind. God Himself is a captive of His "justice" and cannot reverse the effects of Adam's sin. Although Augustine asserts that a small "elect" will be blissfully reunited with God in heaven, even this outcome (which leaves the majority of humanity eternally in hell) is contradicted by his own premises. How could God be reunited in love with a creature who, as Augustine tells us, remains unworthy of His love? How

---

101 Paul Tillich, *A History of Christian Thought* (New York: Harper and Row), p. 128.

could creatures who know they are utterly worthless be open to receiving the love of God?

Insofar as I feel unworthy, I believe that the person who loves me is deluding herself, i.e., that she does not in fact love *me*, but that persona she mistakenly believes me to be. She could not love me because I am not objectively lovable: I am contemptible in the eyes of God. Either she is herself despicable, or she is the victim of a delusion. In either case, to use a metaphor, I can not fully open myself to receiving her love. As Erich Fromm has argued, a fundamental sense of self-worth is a precondition for surrendering to the experience of love.[102] If this is true for love between human beings, it is also true in regard to humanity's acceptance of the love of God. Augustine's vision of an elect living in blissful harmony with God is contradicted by his premise that this elect remains eternally guilty—and aware of its guilt—of a crime for which it never should have been forgiven.

I do not mean to imply, however, that one could ever experience love—let alone God's grace—as *merited*. Love always has a quality of gratuitousness because it is experienced as a gift, as unearned, as a finite creature's experience of the infinite. Human love in the profound sense of the term is experienced as a *divine* benediction since there is always a quality of incommensurability between what I am—a finite creature—and what I have been given— boundless love—through the grace of God. This is also obviously true in the unmediated encounter with God.

If we look at the possibility of reunion from God's side, we find the same problem with Augustine's premises. How could God be satisfied by the love of a *contemptible*

102 Erich Fromm, *The Art of Loving.*

creature? What would occur would be the master-slave dialectic so well described by Hegel.[103] The master yearns for recognition, for confirmation of his being. But once he has posited the other as a slave, as an ontologically deficient being, the recognition ceases to have any value.

Jesus tells his disciples that in the human being in need He himself is present. It is here that Christianity is most at odds with its Augustinian interpretation. The Augustinian cannot see Christ in his brother—he sees a human being who is essentially a worthless sinner, guilty of the most heinous crime against God.

The affirmation of the other as holy is the ontological and anthropological basis for love—at least for the kind of love that Christ commanded us to manifest toward each other. Christ stated, "This is my command, that you love one another as I have loved you" (John 15:12). Any other kind of "love" has no spiritual significance and is merely a biological bond between creatures. Thus Augustinianism impedes the development of the capacity for love since it deprives love of the ontological grounding that is necessary for its growth.

In Augustine's theory the Incarnation is depleted of any genuine significance. The Incarnation makes possible the reunion of God and sinful humanity. Yet for Augustine there is an unbridgeable ontological abyss that lies between man, the defiled criminal, and God, the merciful and just Judge. Therefore there can be no reunion of God and the mass of humanity.

Augustine has elaborated an ontology of deficiency, flaw, and absence. It is an ontology of anti-Being, from

103 See Peter Singer, *Hegel* (New York: Oxford University Press, 1983), pp. 59-62.

which there is no escape. For the masses of the condemned there is no Platonic ideal world to which they can flee—they are trapped forever in Hell. Actually both humanity and God are forever trapped in the slaughterhouse that has been created as a result of Adam's sin. Being manifests itself primarily as suffering, estrangement, and loss. There is really no way back to paradise.

Most poignant of all in Augustine's vision is the absence of God, for the cruel tyrant that Augustine invented is not the loving Father of Jesus. Perhaps Augustine's inspiration for his portrait of God is the egocentric emperors who ruled the Roman Empire, carrying on a continual war against all foreigners, destroying all cities, murdering, raping, and enslaving their victims. The willingness of Augustine's God to consign all His "enemies," even infants, to eternal torment would certainly make Him a war criminal by the standards of the Geneva Convention.

Augustianinism and the Fusion of Church and State

How can we explain the transformation of Christ's diabolical vision of a loving father who delighted in the repentance of the worst sinner—of any sinner—with the Augustinian vision, reaffirmed by Luther and Calvin of a God who predestined the overwhelming majority of humanity to eternal torment in hell? I think this explanation lies in the decision of the Church to accept an alliance with the Roman Emperor in the 4th century.

For several centuries after their Lord and Savior was executed on the cross by the Roman state, Christians remained faithful to the meaning of the cross and were themselves martyred and executed for their refusal to sanction the divine right of kings, to participate in the imperial cult of the emperor, and to confess the Roman emperor as Lord and divinely appointed sovereign. As Pagels notes, "Even worse [to the Romans], they threatened to replace the image of the Emperor as the manifestation of divine power on earth with Jesus, a condemned criminal...an illiterate barbarian executed by the Romans for treason against the state!"[104]

Although Christians obeyed all the laws of the Roman Empire, their religion with its emphasis on the equality of all individuals was subversive to the ideology that undergirded the Roman Empire. Roman officials lived in fear that such incendiary ideas would catch fire among the disaffected, especially among subject nations and slaves. Thus Rome relentlessly persecuted members of the Christian sect.

Until the 4th century Christians lived in continuous conflict with the Roman state. Many Christians had come to question the rationale of monarchy itself. As we have seen, the Christian doctrine that all human beings are equal in the sight of God was implicitly subversive to the divine right of kings.

Until the triumph of Augustinianism one of the themes emphasized most strongly by Christian thinkers and teachers was that human beings had the freedom to sin or not to sin. The whole point of the story of Adam, as Elaine Pagels commented, was to warn people not to misuse the divinely given capacity for free choice. Virtually all of the early Church Fathers believed that insofar as the human being was created in the image of God, he or she had

104 Elaine Pagels, *Adam, Eve and the Serpent* (New York: Random House, 1988), p. 39.

the capacity for free will. It is for this reason, St. John Chrysostom argued, that the priest must not coerce his congregants to act virtuously. He wrote, "The wrongdoer must be corrected not by force, but by persuasion."[105] The Christian leader must respect each member's freedom of conscience. "If a person wanders away from the right path, great effort, perseverance and patience are required; for he can not be dragged back by force...but must be led back by persuasion to the truth from which he originally swerved."[106]

Pagels notes that before the triumph of Augustinianism "the representatives of Christian orthodoxy, from Justin through Irenaeus, Tertullian, Clement, and Origen had denounced Gnostic interpretations of Genesis in the name of moral freedom."[107] She points out how remarkable it was that the majority of Christians in the 5th century could be persuaded to give up this primary theme of Christianity—freedom of the will—following Augustine's reinterpretation of the consequences of Adam's sin.

In the 4th century, when Christianity accepted the patronage of Constantine, who viewed Christianity as a means for unifying his empire, it began to be transformed from a worldview held by a persecuted sect to the religion of the Roman Empire.[108]

Neither Augustine, Luther, nor Calvin had any qualms

---

105 Cited in Ibid., p. 103.
106 Cited in Ibid., p. 103.
107 Ibid., p. 152.
108 Alister Kee argues that Constantine did not really "convert" to Christianity; rather, he recognized the political expediency of a coalition with the Christians. See A. Kee, *Constantine vs. Christ* (London: SCM Press, 1982).

about accepting the support of the government. In fact, Augustine instructed the leaders of his church, "You teach kings to rule for the benefit of their people; and it is you who warn the people to be subservient to their kings."[109] Calvin stated, "We owe an attitude of reverence and therefore of piety toward all our rulers, whatever they be like."[110]

When Augustine became powerful and was supported by the Roman state as the Bishop of Carthage, he advocated laws denying civil rights to non-Catholic Christians, evictions from public office, and finally denial of free discussion, exile of "heretical" bishops, and the use of physical coercion. He came to find military force "indispensable" in suppressing his ideological opponents.[111] Luther and Calvin also found no hesitation in using the power of church and state to suppress dissidents and coerce agreement by violence.

In the face of the barbaric and criminal activities of the Roman Empire, many Christians must have wondered whether they were compromising their own principles by aligning themselves with Constantine, the imperial conqueror.[112] St. John Chrystostom was so ambivalent about this alliance that though he spent six years as spiritual advisor to the emperor, he continually offended virtually everyone within the royal court and was finally expelled from office when he insisted upon building a hospital for lepers

109 Cited in Elaine Pagels, *Adam, Eve and the Serpent*, p. 123.
110 Cited in Wilhelm Niesel, *The Theology of Calvin* (Philadelphia, Pennsylvania: Westminster Press, 1956), p. 128.
111 Pagels, *Adam, Eve and the Serpent*, p. 124.
112 It should be noted that at this point the Church was not motivated by a desire to escape persecution. The edict of Taler passed in the 4th century effectively ended persecution of Christians. Clearly the motivation of the Church was to share in the power of the world.

directly outside the city walls.[113] One historian wrote that Chrystostom "proudly disdained the favor of the court, on which the high position of his episcopate alone rested, by his foolish idealism." Chrystostom died three years later in exile, ill and alone, consoled by only a few loyal friends.[114]

In collaborating with the state the church implicitly or explicitly sanctioned its policies, e.g., war, imperial plunder, slavery, and itself came to emulate these policies as exemplified by the Inquisition. Kee believes that the decision to collaborate with Constantine led to "the Great Reversal." The values of Constantine were deemed to be the values of Christ, were accepted by the Church, and became known as "Christianity."[115] Kee notes that it is in this way that the values of Constantine—disguised as the values of Christianity—determined the subsequent course of European history.

Christ forbad violence against others and advocated love for one's enemies. Kee states ironically, "Does the Emperor wage war on his enemies to destroy them? Then so does God."[116] Mesmerized by Constantine and the lure of worldly power, Christians violated the most fundamental commandments of Jesus. Kee comments, "It is the revelation of Christ that God does not act as do the Kings of the earth....It is a claim that at a profound level reality is completely different from the common view of it."[117] In addition to emulating Constantine in its sanction of and

113 Elaine Pagels, *Adam, Eve and the Serpent*, p. 121.
114 Ibid., p. 122.
115 Alistair Kee, *Constantine vs. Christ*, p. 140.
116 Ibid., p. 143.
117 Ibid., p. 144.

reliance upon coercion and violence, the Church also emu-
lated him in another respect. The imperial model of authority was accepted so that "the princes of the Church
lived in palaces and exercised dominion over an adminis-
trative district,"[118] paralleling the civil administration of
the Empire.

Just as these practices were explicitly contrary to what
Jesus taught, so was the new Christian anthropology constructed by Augustine contrary to the anthropological perspective of Jesus in which all human beings were regarded
as holy, children of God, and in which the person at the
bottom of the social hierarchy, the one who was hungry or
needy, was deemed to be a manifestation of Jesus Christ
Himself. Thus Augustine's misanthropic anthropology—
which held that the mass of human beings were so depraved that they could not be persuaded to turn from the
path of heresy without coercion—provided the deep-structure that made it appear as if violence, coercion, slavery,
domination, the accumulation of excessive wealth, and the
collaboration of the Church and the State were legitimate
means for the advancement of the cause of Christianity.

Augustinianism

It may be helpful to summarize the salient philosophical premises of Augustinianism. First, Augustinianism posits that human beings at present are lacking in intrinsic
worth and have lost the capacity to freely choose between
good and evil.

Second, the situation was not what was originally

118 Ibid., p. 163.

intended. Human beings were created worthy: They were innocent and good. They were deserving of God's love. But then a dramatic event occurred—in Augustine's version, Adam's sin destroyed the pristine plenitude of being, bringing tragedy in its wake. The paradise that man inhabited was transformed into a Hell; man was transformed from a godlike being into a vile wretch.

Third, mankind is now divided into two groups: an elect destined by God to be rescued from its plight and restored to its original condition (Augustine's theory implies that the restoration is only partial, since he states that after the crime human beings remain permanently ontologically deficient, i.e., deserving of eternal torment), and the masses doomed to eternal torment in Hell.

Fourth, the transcendence of God is emphasized to the highest degree and stands in marked contrast to the depravity of human beings. This is the core premise of Augustinianism and has had an enduring effect upon Christianity and upon culture: There is an unbridgeable ontological abyss between God and humanity. God is totally Other: Human beings have no right to seek to understand Him or to judge Him by human standards. Whatever He does is right merely because He does it. There is no longer a kinship between man and God, no affinity, no similarity that could provide a basis for communion. God is totally Other to man, and man is totally Other to God.

Fifth, Augustinian theorists' writings reveal that they are personally burdened by a disturbing sense of sin, guilt, and unworthiness. They are preoccupied with the question of how to relieve their sense of ontological deficiency. This preoccupation led both Augustine and Luther to misread Paul and to filter the Pauline text through "the dilemma of the introspective conscience of the West."[119]

Sixth, the preoccupation with sin, guilt, and unworthiness leads to an individualistic vision of salvation antithetical to the Christian vision of a new social and cosmic order where the estrangement between human beings, and between human beings and God, is overcome. The Christian vision is eclipsed, and the individual becomes preoccupied with recovering his sense of self-esteem and seeking reassurance that he will be spared the punishment of eternal torment in Hell.

119 Krister Stendahl, *Paul Among Jews and Christians* (Philadelphia, Pennsylvania: Fortress Press, 1976), p. 83.

CHAPTER 3

Augustine and the Emergence of a Western Guilt Culture

Although St. Augustine's influence on Latin Christianity was unparalleled for centuries, the Catholic Church in the 5th century rejected a central tenet of his theology: predestination to damnation. Instead, they promised that those who conformed to the Church's rules would be saved.

Nevertheless there was a recrudescence of Augustinianism in the Catholic Church beginning in the 15th century, and later more significantly with the Protestant Reformation. Jean Delumeau writes that "Augustinian pessimism gained both its strongest coloring and widest audience during the period highlighted by this study, the years 1400 to 1700....It is no exaggeration to assert the debate over original sin and its diverse by-products—problems of grace, free will or servitude, and predestination—came to be one of the prime obsessions of Western civilization, a concern of all people, from the theologians to the most modest peasants."[120] Delumeau notes that many of these Augustinians were even more extremely pessimistic than Augustine himself, for he at least acknowledged some of the noble traits that human beings still possessed.

Delumeau describes the "collective guilt complex"

---

120 Jean Delumeau, *Sin and Fear; the Emergence of a Western Guilt Culture, 13th to 18th Century* (New York: St. Martin's Press, 1990), p. 248.

stemming from Augustine, which he argues dominated Western culture between the 13th and 18th centuries: "A terrible God, more a judge than a father, despite the mercy with which He was almost accidentally credited; a divine justice connected to vengeance; the conviction that, despite Redemption, there would remain only a chosen few, all humanity having deserved hellfire because of Original Sin; the certainty that each sin is both insult and injury to God; the rejection of any amusement or concession to human nature, since these remove one from salvation."[121]

With the displacement of Christ's optimistic ontology by Augustine's pessimistic ontology, the original Judeo-Christian expectation of cosmic redemption, of the divine victory over the forces of evil, of the eventual realization of the Kingdom of God on earth was almost entirely obscured.

Luther: the Regenerate Augustinian

Both Luther and Calvin were staunch admirers of Augustine, believing that his legacy had been besmirched by the Catholic Church. Their theologies were consequently based on a reassertion of Augustinian anthropology.

It is well known that Luther's apostasy from Roman Catholicism and his development of the concept of "justification by faith" was the denouement of his unsuccessful struggle as an Augustinian monk to attain to a sense of sinlessness, in which he could be assured that he had attained the favor of God. Despite all the austerities Luther imposed upon himself, he was ultimately left with a sense of his own depravity. From this he deduced that man was

121 Ibid., p. 296.

inherently depraved and as a result could do nothing by his own works to earn the forgiveness of God.

Shortly before Luther's conversion he prayed, "With what tongue shall I address such Majesty, seeing that all men ought to tremble in the presence of even an earthly prince? Who am I that I should lift up mine eyes or raise my hands to the divine Majesty?...And shall I, a miserable little pygmy, say 'I want this, I ask for that?' For I am dust and ashes and full of sin."[122]

Like Augustine, Luther believed that man incurred both the guilt for Adam's sin in paradise and the disease of that sin as it was passed on through the act of procreation. He wrote, "I am a sinner, not because I have committed adultery nor because I have had Uriah murdered, but I have committed adultery and murder because I was born, indeed conceived and formed in the womb, as a sinner....So we are not sinners because we commit this or that sin, but we commit them because we are sinners first. That is, a bad tree and a bad seed also bring forth bad fruits, and from a bad root only a bad tree can grow." The image of God that Adam had borne in his soul was replaced by "the image of the devil."[123] This entailed a "corruption of the whole nature and of all the powers of man...a corruption which infects the mind, intellect, heart and will."[124] (Lutherans, after Luther, were reluctant to construe corruption as pervasively as their teacher had.)

122 Cited in William A. Scott, *Historical Protestantism: An Historical Introduction to Protestant Theory* (Englewood Cliffs, New Jersey: Prentice-Hall, 1970), p. 3.

123 Luther cited in Jaroslav Pelikan, *The Reformation of the Church and Dogma, 1300-1700*, Volume 4 (Chicago: University of Chicago Press, 1988), p. 142.

124 N.P. Williams, *The Idea of the Fall and of Original Sin*, p. 429.

But even worse than the corruption of sin itself is the wrath of God that it incurred, bringing as it did the curse of God and the punishment of death. Since God was eternal and omnipotent, "His fury or wrath toward self-satisfied sinners is also immeasurable and infinite."[125] This divine "justice" created "horrible torments of the heart and fury of conscience."[126] In these torments or "terrors of the conscience that feels God's wrath against our sins and looks for forgiveness of sins and deliverance from sin,"[127] it was worse than useless to lay claim to merit by doing good deeds in an attempt to win God's favor.

Luther struggled with Paul's phrase in the Epistle to the Romans that "the just shall live by His faith." He was relieved of his torments one day when an epiphany occurred to him: "Then I grasped that the justice of God is that righteousness by which through grace and sheer mercy God justifies us through faith. Thereupon I felt myself to be reborn and to have gone through open doors into paradise."[128]

Luther had originally grasped God as a wrathful judge, but the good news that he now realized was that God had expended his punitive justice on Christ, that by His death Christ had taken upon Himself the guilt of man, thereby satisfying God's punitive justice.[129] This is what Luther means by justification: that human beings' sins are

<hr/>

125 Luther, cited in Jarosalv Pelikan, *The Reformation of the Church and Dogma, 1300-1700*, Volume 4, p. 132.

126 Ibid., p. 133.

127 Ibid., p. 133.

128 William A. Scott, *Historical Protestantism: An Historical Introduction to Protestant Theory*, p. 7.

129 Ibid., p. 7.

forgiven. However, they remain in the bondage of sin. God forgives sinners and reckons them as "righteous" for Christ's sake. Thus the righteousness granted to the sinner is not one produced by himself but an "alien" righteousness belonging to Jesus Christ. It is a righteousness "outside of" man; it is not a quality of man's heart.[130] In order to receive this justification human beings must believe in Jesus Christ. Although God justifies the individual, he remains throughout his life a sinner. Therefore Luther described him as "righteous and a sinner at the same time [simul justus et peccator]."[131]

Luther's position parallels Augustine's: Although man is acquitted of the guilt for Adam's crime, he remains a sinner and damnable before God. Luther does believe that subsequent to justification God works to "sanctify the believer," so that after death he will be worthy of entering into communion with Christ.

There were tendencies in Luther's thought that were not as entirely pessimistic. Thus, although he asserted frequently that the image of God in man had been completely destroyed,[132] in several passages he writes of a relic that remains. The relic consists wholly in man's "natural" abilities, in his difference from animals, which gives him the power to govern things.[133] Thus Luther writes that we have "the blunted and as it were dead relics of their [Adam's

130 Paul Althaus, *The Theology of Martin Luther* (Philadelphia, Pennsylvania: Fortress Press, 1966), p. 288.
131 Jaroslav Pelikan, *The Reformation of the Church and Dogma, 1300-1700*, Volume 4, p. 154.
132 David Cairns, *The Image of God in Man* (London: SCM Press, 1953), p. 24.
133 Ibid., p. 126.

and Eve's] knowledge."[134] The image in the sense of goodness and justice was totally destroyed.[135] Sin, however, does
not destroy human beings' capacity to be grasped by God's
grace; otherwise salvation would be impossible.

Like Augustine, Luther denied that God willed the
salvation of all human beings, and he asserted that he
"saved so few and damned so many."[136] Luther's explanation for this is similar to that of Augustine: By not grant-
ing salvation to all, God shows us that His grace can not
be taken for granted. By rejecting so many He shows us
that His mercy is a free act of His will. Luther assures us
that we have no rights in relation to God; on the contrary,
He has every right to do what He wants. He owes us nothing. Like Augustine, Luther conceived God as a majestic
sovereign, to whose arbitrary fiat human beings—at least
those who are predestined to be saved—ought to succumb
in fear, in reverence, and in gratitude.

Luther asserted that original sin had completely ab-
negated freedom of the will, which was now entirely in
bondage to sin, and "not free to strive toward whatever is
declared good."[137] He stated that man "neither does the
good nor is capable of it in the absence of grace."[138] Luther's
opponents accused him of forbidding good works. He responded that he had only denied both that good works
would contribute to man's salvation, and that they were a
product of man's free will. On the other hand, he did not

134 See David Cairns, *Image of God in Man* (London: SCM Press,
1953), p. 122.
135 Ibid., p. 122.
136 Paul Althaus, *The Theology of Martin Luther*, p. 279.
137 Luther, cited in Jaroslav Pelikan, *The Reformation of Church
and Dogma*, p. 141.
138 Ibid., p. 141.

deny that good works were a product of grace and faith.

Good deeds that are done by those who are not baptized are not really good at all. Thus, speaking of the Jews, Luther said, "Men truly sin even when they perform good works apart from the Holy Spirit."[139] Thus all of man's moral aspirations and accomplishments, apart from Christianity, are stigmatized by Luther as corrupt and worthless in the sight of God. Luther acknowledges that human beings possess "heroic virtues" and that we can find copious evidence in society of "civil righteousness." Yet he maintains that this righteousness is honored only by men and not by God, and that it constitutes a kind of false front for "the truth in our inward being" is missing.[140]

This concept is a product of Luther's rendering of original sin. As long as original sin exists in the human being—as long as the consequences are not mitigated by grace—even the most altruistic and noble deeds of human beings are really manifestations of the crime and the disease of original sin. Luther wrote, "Our weakness lies not in our works but in our nature; our person, nature, and entire being are corrupted through Adam's fall....There is simply nothing in us which is not sinful."[141] Only God can liberate humankind from this condition. (Of course He restricts this liberation to the elect.)

139 Cited in N.P. Williams, *The Idea of the Fall and of Original Sin*, p. 431.
140 Cited in Paul Althaus, *The Theology of Martin Luther*, p. 144.
141 Ibid., p. 153.

CHAPTER 4

Calvin and Total Depravity

Like Augustine and Luther, Calvin believed that man's nature was altered and irreparably damaged by original sin. He stated, "Infants bring their own damnation with them from their mothers' wombs; the moment they are born, their natures are odious and abominable to God."[142] Self-knowledge leads to self-contempt, which for Calvin is the true way to find God. "Self-knowledge progresses most when one is crushed and abashed by one's own calamity, poverty, nudity and ignominy, for there is no danger that man can go too far in abasing himself."[143] In the process of self-abasement man stands to discover "in God that which is missing in himself."[144]

Calvin wrote, "As a result of the Fall there is an impassable gulf between humanity and God which only God can bridge. How could man help himself when by the shameful Fall he was degraded to death and Hell, sullied with so many stains, fetid with his corruption and wholly in the power of the curse?"[145]

Man is not only born guilty in God's sight, but he is tainted by the semen from which he is descended. Calvin

---

142 Cited in N.P. Williams, *The Ideas of the Fall and of Original Sin*, p. 432.

143 Jean Delumeau, *Sin and Fear: The Emergence of a Western Guilt Culture, 13th-18th Centuries*, p. 29.

144 Ibid., p. 29.

145 Wilhelm Niesel, *The Theology of Calvin* (Philadelphia, Pennsylvania: Westminster Press, 1956), p. 112.

wrote, "Therefore all of us, who have descended from impure seed, are born infected with the contagion of sin. In fact, before we saw the light of this life we were soiled and spotted in God's sight. 'For who can bring a clean thing from an unclean?' as the book of Job says (Job 14:4)."[146]

All of creation has been deformed by original sin. "No matter where we look, high or low, we can see only a curse that, spreading over all creatures and embracing the earth and the sky, ought to burden our souls with horrible despair."[147]

According to Calvin, as a result of original sin human beings no longer possess the capacity to do good. He stated, "We are all sinners by nature: it thus follows that we live beneath the yoke of sin. Now if all men are held captive by sin, the will which is man's primary characteristic, must need to be clasped and enclosed in tight fetters by Satan....We are nothing but sin"—unless the sovereign grace of God frees us from ourselves.[148]

While Calvin asserted the doctrine of total depravity, he also denied that the image of God had been completely destroyed by the Fall. In one passage he asserts, "The Lord enjoins us to do good to all without exception, though the greater part, if estimated by their own merit, are unworthy of it. The Scripture enjoined a most excellent reason when it tells us that we are not to look to what men themselves deserve, but to the image of God, which exists in all, and to which we owe all honor and love...."[149]

146 Jean Delumeau, *Sin and Fear: the Emergence of a Western Guilt Culture, 13th to 18th Century*, p. 499.

147 Cited in Ibid., p. 29.

148 Cited in Ibid., p. 536.

149 Cited in David Cairns, *The Image of God in Man* (London: SCM Press, 1953), p. 139.

This passage seems to attribute an intrinsic dignity to man, which is uncharacteristic of Calvin. For the most part his doctrine of the remaining "remnants" of the image is meant to explain the existence of natural gifts in man, and is thus in accord with Augustine's theory. Calvin argues that man's natural abilities include a residue of intelligence and judgment, although soundness of mind and integrity of heart are withdrawn after the Fall.[150] Cairns writes, paraphrasing Calvin, "Some sparks remain in man to show that he is a rational animal, different from the brutes, but this light is almost smothered by clouds of darkness."[151]

The bulk of the passages on the surviving remnants of the image of God cannot be reconciled with the idea that human beings retain a quality of intrinsic worthiness. Calvin states, "Even though we grant that God's image was not totally annihilated and destroyed in him, yet it is so corrupted that whatever remains is frightful deformity." In another passage Calvin writes, "There is more worth in all the vermin in the world than in man, for he is a creature where the image of God has been effaced and where the good which God has put in it has been corrupted. There is nothing in him but sin...."[152]

Calvin developed a doctrine of "double predestination." While all men were deserving of damnation, some, due to no merit of their own, were saved. He criticized the Lutheran view, which referred only to predestination of those who were elected to salvation. Those who are not elected God "passes over," but this must be because He *condemns* them, "and this He does for no other reason than

150 Ibid., p. 136.
151 Ibid., p. 136.
152 Cited in David Cairns, *The Image of God in Man*, p. 139.

that He wills to exclude them from the inheritance that He predestines for His own children."[153] As Pelikan notes, for Calvin reprobation to damnation by the eternal will of God was an ineluctable corollary of election to salvation by the same will.[154]

To his opponents, who argued that Calvin had painted a portrait of an unjust God who arbitrarily decided to save some and to damn others, Calvin responded that "whatever He wills by the very fact that He wills it must be considered righteous."[155] He stated that this was a mystery beyond man's comprehension, and he insisted that the justice of God and double predestination was a subject "to adore rather than to scrutinize."[156]

Yet Calvin himself apparently had ambivalent feelings about the justice of God's will. He stated, "I inquire again how it came to pass that the fall of Adam, independent of any remedy, should involve so many nations with their infant children in eternal death, but because such was the will of God...it is an awful decree, I confess!"[157]

Calvin affirmed Luther's doctrine that when a man is justified by God he remains a sinner and yet just, because in Christ God imputes justice to him. Baptism is a sign that human beings are freed both from the guilt that "should have been imputed to us [as a result of original

153 Cited in Jaroslav Pelikan, *The Reformation of the Church and Dogma, 1300-1700* (Chicago: University of Chicago Press, 1984), Volume 4, p. 222.

154 Cited in Ibid., p. 222.

155 Cited in William A. Scott, *Historical Protestantism: An Historical Introduction to Protestant Theory* (Englewood Cliffs, New Jersey: Prentice-Hall, 1970), p. 39.

156 Cited in Jaroslav Pelikan, *The Reformation of the Church and Dogma, 1300-1700*, Volume 4, p. 231.

sin] and the punishment that we ought to have undergone because of the guilt."[158] However, it does not deliver us "from original sin and from the corruption which is descended from Adam to all his posterity."[159] (Again, there is no explanation for why human beings bear the guilt for an act that Calvin had asserted was predestined by God!)

The Penal Theory of Atonement

The enduring influence of Augustine, Calvin and Luther on modern culture in general, and on Christianity in particular, continues to this day. Although Augustinianism's influence on Christianity waned in the 19th century with the burgeoning of Enlightenment thought and the establishment of the democratic idea, evangelical Christianity incorporated some Augustinian elements through Calvinism and Lutheranism.

Although the sacrificial theory of atonement was first articulated only in the 11th century, by Anselm of Canterbury, and reformulated in the 19th century by the Evangelical Christian Charles Hodge, Anselm's explanation for the atonement was based on a traditional Augustinian concept of God. This concept of salvation was yet another example of Augustine's corrupting influence on Christianity. Since sin is an offense to the "honor" of God, God has to punish people or have them offer "satisfaction" to make amends for the offenses committed. In order to satisfy

157 Cited in Paul Tillich, *A History of Christian Thought* (New York: Simon and Schuster, 1968), p. 268.

158 Cited in William A. Scott, *Historical Protestantism: An Historical Introduction to Protestant Theory*, p. 146.

159 Ibid., p. 46.

God's justice, Christ agreed to die on the cross in substitute for sinful human beings. Christ's death is an act of obedience that outweighs humanity's sinful acts and therefore merited God's reward. Since Christ did not need God's reward, He passed it on to humanity, thus allowing God to forgive us for our sins.[160] In Hodge's version God is a prosecutor or a judge who is satisfied only when the punishment rightly deserved by mankind has been discharged.

Clark Pinnock and Robert Brow argue that this theory has been a major obstacle to the understanding of Christianity: "It demotes the resurrection from its central place and changes the cross from scandal to abstract theory. It makes things sound as if God *wanted* Jesus to die....Surely not. Jesus is God's beloved Son, the Father and the Son are not divided or in opposition....Before the cross happened, God loved sinners and wanted to save them. The cross did not purchase love for sinners. It is we, not God, who need to be changed in attitude."[161]

The penal theory is not without deep biblical resonances in the Old Testament's depiction of God's wrath, but it is certainly inconsistent with the essential message of Christ's gospel, that God's offer of salvation was extended to all. As Clark Pinnock puts it, "The decisive element in Jesus' teaching and acting was communication of the boundlessness of God's grace to sinners."[162] As Jesus stated, "I tell you...there will be more rejoicing in Heaven

160 See Ibid., pp. 51-52.
161 Clark Pinnock and Robert Brow, *Unbounded Love* (Downers Grove, Illinois: InterVarsity Press, 1994), pp. 102-103.
162 Clark Pinnock, *A Wideness in God's Mercy* (Downers Grove, Illinois: InterVarsity Press, 1992), p. 31.

over one sinner who repents than over ninety-nine righteous persons who do not need to repent." (Luke 15:7) Or in Michael Winter's words, "In Jesus' own dealings with sinners and in His teaching about forgiveness, compensation is never required as a prior condition for being received back into the love of God. This is true of the parables of forgiveness, the narratives of conversion or reconciliation of individuals or in the plain teachings of Christ. Satisfaction is never required as a condition of their being reconciled with God the Father."[163]

In the parable of the prodigal son (Luke 15:11-32), the son is accepted by his father even though he does not repay him the money he squandered. In Matthew 8:21-22 Peter asks Jesus how often he should forgive his brother ("Should it be up to seven times?"), and Jesus replies, "Until seventy times seven." He makes no mention of prior compensation. Even on the cross, as sinners drive nails through His hands, Jesus says, "Father, forgive them." The goal of the Father is a reconciled human community—the new covenant of Christ. The means to this goal is forgiveness and repentance, not retribution and compensation. What God asks of human beings is certainly not less than He is willing to give Himself. In Matthew 6:14, after reciting the Lord's Prayer, Christ explicitly states, "For if you forgive men when they sin against you, your Heavenly Father will also forgive you."

Advocates of penal atonement sometimes insist that because God is just He *must* grant justice and punish transgression. But as Christos Yannaras, the Greek Orthodox

---

163 Michael Winter, *The Atonement* (Collegeville, Minnesota: Liturgical Press, 1995), p. 66.

theologian, asks:

> But from what do they derive this "must" to which they
> subordinate even God? Does there exist, then, some
> necessity that limits the love of God, limits His free-
> dom? If there is, then God is not God or at least He is
> not the God that the Church knows. A "just" God, a
> heavenly police constable who oversees the keeping of
> the laws of an obligatory—even for Him—justice is just
> a figment of the imagination of fallen humanity, a pro-
> jection of its need for a supernatural individual secu-
> rity within the reciprocal treachery of collective co-
> existence...."As a grain of sand can not counterbalance
> a great quantity of gold, so in comparison God's use of
> justice can not counterbalance His mercy," says St. Isaac
> the Syrian.[164]

I am not of course denying that Christ's death was a
voluntary sacrifice undergone for the salvation of humanity. On this fact the biblical witness is unequivocal. But the
point is that the Western, Roman Catholic-Evangelical penal satisfaction theory of atonement is an inadequate explanation for the efficacy of Christ's mission, death, and
resurrection. It exaggerates the gulf that exists between
humanity and God by depicting the human being as Sinner and God as the Judge, and it violates the biblical witness to God as the Father who desires the restoration of
communion with and among His sons and daughters. It
reflects an Augustinian preoccupation with guilt and ontological deficiency, and it assumes that the whole purpose of Christ's work was merely to secure individuals'

164 Christos Yannaras, *Elements of Christian Faith: An Introduction to Orthodox Theology* (Minneapolis, Minnesota: Light and Life Publishers, 1997), p. 83.

legal acquittal in the heavenly tribunal, thus partially miti-
gating their ontological deficiency and sparing them from
the torments of eternal Hell. This is an impoverished conception of redemption that eschews its social, political, and
cosmic implications.

A corollary to the penal atonement theory is a conception of faith that is entirely nonbiblical. Justification is
reduced to a private transaction between the individual
and God. Faith is defined as a passive acceptance of the
fact that one is a sinner and Christ is one's savior. On the
basis of this passive acceptance one is declared legally righteous by God. "Christ's righteousness is imputed to the
sinner in a forensic or legal sense, even though one does
not yet display righteousness or holiness of character."[165]
This view is in conflict with the biblical concept of faith,
justification, and righteousness, all of which are means not
simply to expiate the individual's guilt but to create and
sustain a community that conforms to a "new social-spiri-
tual order of human relationships under the authority of
God,"[166] and a community that lives in communion with
God.

Faith is understood by Paul not as the passive acceptance that one is a sinner saved by Christ, but as an attitude that is instrumental in bringing about the reconciliation of humanity and God: "For Paul, Abraham is the classic example of faith. In Romans 4 (cf. Hebrews 11:8-19),
Abraham's faith is described as a continuing attitude of
trust in the face of seemingly insurmountable difficulties

---

165 John Driver, *Understanding the Atonement for the Mission of
the Church* (Scottdale, Pennsylvania: Herald Press, 1986), p. 199.

166 C. Norman Kraus, *Jesus Christ Our Lord* (Scottdale, Pennsylvania: Herald Press, 1990), p. 241.

and temptation to despair....So like the Old Testament concept of *emunah* [faith], Abraham's faith was a matter of attitude *and* conduct."[167]

It is beyond the scope of this book to examine the various theories of atonement. (Such a "fully-orbed Biblical perspective" is provided by Driver, who takes into account all of the dimensions of the atonement, e.g., expiation, sacrifice, intercession, etc.) The point here is merely to show how *certain* Augustinian deformations of Christianity (1) conflict with scriptural witness and (2) lead to an acceptance of the status quo, and a capitulation to the powers of this world, and thus prevent us from understanding the Church as a force for transformation in a world in bondage to sin and death.

Although Augustinianism is associated with an epoch that the modern world is believed to have long transcended, it will be shown in the following chapters that the Augustinian narrative, along with its root metaphor of the irreparably damaged soul, retained its hold upon the collective imagination—it merely clothed itself in secular garb suited to the fashion of modern times. The philosophies of the Enlightenment were generally optimistic and thus presented a stumbling block to Augustinianism, with its bleak vision of human possibility. However, Augustinianism had sunk its roots deep into the collective imagination of Western humanity, and it was not destined to fade away.

At the beginning of the 20th century, its theology was re-presented as psychological science and introduced to the modern world as a bold new discovery about the

167 John Driver, *Understanding the Atonement for the Mission of the Church*, p. 199.

nature of the human mind based on the investigations of the master of depth psychology, Dr. Sigmund Freud.

PART TWO

CHAPTER 5

The Myth of Mental Illness: Freud's Secularization of Augustine's Metaphysics

As a graduate student, I defined myself as a revisionist Freudian, a neo-psychoanalyst, and subscribed to the dogmas that were then and now held by most in the psychoanalytic professions. (Many "orthodox" Freudian dogmas, e.g., the centrality of the Oedipal complex in the individual's life, have been abandoned by most psychoanalysts.) On my own initiative I underwent psychoanalytic therapy for three years as an adolescent, and for two years in graduate school. (I do not think it contributed much one way or the other to my emotional-spiritual development.) I studied psychoanalytic theory extensively, both in my Masters Program (1976-1978) and in my Doctoral Program (1980-1984). In 1979, 1981-2 and 1985-6, after I had completed my doctorate, I practiced "psychoanalytic therapy" under the tutelage respectively of three Freudian psychologists.

In 1985 I became fascinated by what struck me as a remarkable similarity between the Augustinian version of the myth of the Fall and Freudian theory—both in its "orthodox" and its more modern versions. I wrote about this in several essays.[168] While working on this book, I discov-

168 See, for example, Seth Farber, "Transcending Medicalism: An Evolutionary Alternative," *The Journal of Mind and Behavior*, Winter

ered Richard Webster's book *Why Freud Was Wrong*,[169] in which he also points to the Augustinian character of Freud's project. This corroborated my own argument.

As Webster notes, Freud confidently proclaimed that psychoanalysis had inflicted the "second great blow on the naive self-love of man." The first blow had been inflicted by Darwin, who proved "man's ineradicable animal nature."[170] Webster points out that Augustine was probably the first seminal thinker in Western civilization to develop a misanthropic anthropology. What Freud did was to recast Augustinian ideas about the depravity of human beings in "scientific" secular garb, thus making them more palatable in a civilization that was repudiating religion and embracing secularized ideals. As Thomas Szasz noted, Science is the religion of secular men and women—the source of Authority—in the 20th century.

Webster eloquently describes the dilemma Freud found himself in the light of his project to puncture man's self-esteem: "In the intellectual environment of 19th century Vienna Freud found himself in a cultural predicament. With certain significant exceptions, the intellectual climate was one of assumed rational optimism. Animal appetites and all forms of sexual behavior were treated as animal residues of a nature which would eventually be refined—

1987, Volume VIII, Number 1, and Seth Farber, "The Image of God: A Summons to the Good Fight," *The Christian Activist*, Volume V, 1995, pps. 30-37. In the latter essay I distinguished the Augustinian interpretation of the myth of the Fall from that of the entirely different Eastern Orthodox interpretation.

169   Richard Webster, *Why Freud Was Wrong* (New York: Basic Books, 1995).

170   Cited in Ibid., p. 314.

by science—into pure rationality.[171] Freud succeeded in undermining this rational optimism in two ways. First, he promulgated a doctrine about the human psyche that was profoundly disturbing and gloomy. As Freud wrote, "Our mind is no peacefully self-contained unity. It is rather to be compared with a modern state in which a mob, eager for enjoyment and destruction, has to be held down by a prudent superior class."[172] Second, he universalized the idea of "mental illness" so that any form of behavior that was caused by emotional conflict was *ipso facto* a form of illness. In accomplishing these tasks, Freud succeeded in carving out a place for himself in the imagination of modern secular man as a Messiah of the 20th century, and in establishing psychoanalysis as a new religion based on Science as the modality for salvation for those who have rejected traditional religion.

Webster's assessment of the climate in which Freud lived as one of "assumed rational optimism" was accurate, as Freud's own picture of Freud and Darwin jointly battling the forces of naive humanism suggests. However, this needs to be qualified: Anti-Semitism in Europe at the turn of the century was rampant in intellectual circles. Its primary theoretical locus was in "medical and biological science," the corpus of the very profession into which Freud aspired to become assimilated.

The traits that Augustine has deemed characteristic of humanity were particularized by European racialist science at the turn of the century and attributed to Jews: (1) that they ostensibly had a propensity for developing physical and mental illnesses, i.e., they were diseased or tainted;

171 Ibid., p. 317.
172 Cited in Ibid., p. 319.

and (2) they had a proclivity to commit crimes, particularly crimes of a sexual nature. Furthermore, they had a tendency to engage in inbreeding—which supposedly led to "degeneracy"—and in engaging in sibling incest. Sanford Gilman's path-breaking work demonstrates that Freud—obviously well acquainted with the racist medical science of his times, although he makes no reference to it in his writing—appropriated the negative traits predicated of the Jews and "universalized" them.

Gilman writes, "For the non-Jewish scientist, the Jew was different, and this difference presented itself as a disease, a disease that affected the Jew directly but could also affect the culture in which the diseased Jew dwelled."[173]The Jewish philosopher Ludwig Wittenstein observed that within European history Jews "are experienced as a kind of disease, an anomaly, and nobody wants to put a disease on the same level as normal life."[174]

Freud commented in a letter to Romain Roland after World War I that, "I, of course, belong to a race which in the Middle Ages was held responsible for all epidemics and which today is blamed for the disintegration of the Austrian Empire and the German defeat."[175] Gilman astutely notes, "The reversal and extension of this view, that the diseases of the Jew are transmuted into the diseases of all human beings, is one of the underlying mechanisms in the establishment of the discourse of psychoanalysis."[176]

Freud's response to the ideas that Jews had a tendency

173 Sanford Gilman, *The Case of Sigmund Freud, Medicine and Identity at the Fin de Siêcle* (Baltimore, Maryland: John Hopkins University Press, 1993).
174 Cited in Ibid., p. 225.
175 Ibid., p. 25.
176 Ibid., p. 25.

to engage in criminal behavior and in sibling incest was that all human beings were incestuous and criminally inclined. "Freud projected the charges of sexual license made against the Jews into primeval history, seeing the original crime, the murder of the father by his sons, as the psychological root of human nature."[177]

Freud's disciple Wilhelm Stekel put it well when he stated that psychoanalysis asserted the latent "universal criminality" of all human beings.[178] Freud translated the charge made against the Jews of brother-sister incest into mother-son incest (which was not one of the charges made against the Jews), and he adds to this the murder of the father.[179] (Of course, for Freud, these crimes take place in the psychic world, not in reality—except for the primeval crime alluded to above.)

If we combine Gilman's perspective with that of Webster, we realize that Freudianism constitutes on the one hand a recrudescence of the Augustinian vision in secular form, and on the other hand an attempt to universalize the (Augustinian) motifs of "original sin," disease, and crime that had been appropriated in a blatantly racist fashion by medical scientists at the end of the 19th century. I am *not* suggesting that intellectual racists of the 19th century were directly influenced by Augustine, but certainly the ideas of Luther and Calvin were well known and had a powerful influence on the culture of Europe before the Enlightenment, as Delumeau has shown.[180] Thus psychoanalysis was both a reaction to the rational optimism of

177   Ibid., p. 199.
178   Ibid., p. 202.
179   Ibid., p. 206.
180   Jean Delumeau, *Sin and Fear: The Emergence of a Western Guilt Culture 13th-19th Century* (New York: St. Martin's Press, 1990).

THE MYTH OF MENTAL ILLNESS

the Enlightenment and to anti-Semitic intellectual currents. By universalizing the traits attributed to the Jews—rather than rejecting them altogether—Freud showed how influenced he was psychologically and intellectually (unconsciously, if not consciously) by the anti-Semitism of his time. Furthermore, even his universalism (like Augustine's) was only partial, since Freud introduced a new bifurcation of the elect and the reprobate: this time not along racial or anti-Semitic lines, but upon lines drawn by the psychoanalytic elite. The reprobate, as will be seen below, were those who were deemed unsusceptible to Freudian psychoanalysis.

The Oedipal Complex—the Little Criminal

For Freud the critical events in the individual's life are those centering around the Oedipal complex. It is no exaggeration to say that for Freud these were the most important events in the individual's life, determining and limiting his or her subsequent development. For both male and female the relationship with the mother remains paramount, and all subsequent love choices are merely unconscious, futile attempts to recapture the intensity of the bonding with "the first and strongest love-object...the prototype of all later love relations."[181] This intimacy is disturbed during the Oedipal stage and is ruptured at its conclusion at age five, when the instinctual desires for the mother are repressed.[182]

181 Sigmund Freud, James. S. Striachey, ed. *Outline of Psychoanalysis* (New York: W.W. Norton and Company, 1989), p. 71.
182 According to Freud, the Oedipal complex reaches its height for the male child when, at two or three years of age, he develops the

CHAPTER FIVE

Freud did not regard children as innocent in the non-legal or romantic sense of the term. Since they had not committed any crime, they were not guilty in the legal (Augustinian) sense, but since if they had the power to satisfy their instincts they would have done so, they were "evil." Freud wrote, "The impulses...subjected to repression are those of selfishness and cruelty, which can be summed up in general as evil, but above all sexual wishful impulses,

fantasy of becoming his mother's lover and "he tries to seduce her by showing her the male organ which he is proud to own" (Ibid., p. 71). At the same time he develops hostility to his father as a "rival who stands in the way and whom he would like to get rid of" (Ibid., p. 71). Freud commends the 18th century philosopher Diderot for his foresight when he wrote, "If the little savage were left to himself, preserving all his foolishness and adding to the small sense of a child in the cradle the violent passions of a man of thirty, he would strangle his father and lie with his mother" (Ibid., p. 75). The child experiences the threat of castration, which is evoked either by explicit or implicit threat by the mother or father and by his recall or observation of female genitals—this is "the severest trauma of his young life" (Ibid., p. 72). Freud also states that the threat has added potency from the child's phylogenetic memory traces "from the pre-history of the primal family, when the jealous father actually robbed his son of his genitals if the latter became troublesome to him as a rival with a woman" (Ibid., p. 72). This leads to the repression of his Oedipal feelings: his desire for his mother, and his homicidal feelings toward his father. Because the child also has affection for his father, he develops a sense of guilt for his aggressive desires. The father is internalized into his psyche and becomes the basis of the Superego, which from that moment onward exercises vigilance to ensure that the repressed desires, which are never extinguished, do not return. The female also renounces her Oedipal attachment to her mother (at approximately the same age as the boy), although the trajectory is obviously different from that of the male child. The girl, comparing herself to the male, "under the influence of her envy for the penis, cannot forgive her mother for having sent her into the world so insufficiently often of the crudest and most forbidden kind."[183] He wrote that we overlook the "frightful evil" that is manifest in children "on account of their small size."[184] As David McClelland, a Quaker sympathetic to psychoanalysis, wrote of Freud's most prominent disciple, his daughter Anna, "In fact, to hear Anna Freud speak of the criminal tendencies of the one- and two-year-old is to be reminded inevitably of Calvinistic sermons on infant damnation."[185]

The Universal Neurosis

But it was the idea of mental disease more than that of evil that dominated Freud's mind. As Webster points out, originally Freud assumed that there was a small group of neurotics who had developed their pathology as a result of being sexually abused as children, but by the time he developed his Oedipal theory he had decided that neurosis was a universal phenomenon (that was not caused by parental actions).[186]

equipped." Bitterly ashamed of her "stunted penis" (Ibid., p. 76) and resentful against her mother, she transfers her love to her father and identifies with her mother as a means of compensating for the loss of her mother as a love-object. At first she desires to possess the father's penis, but in "normal" development this is transferred into the wish to have a baby from the father. The longing to possess a penis remains and is "unappeasable," but the woman may find satisfaction "if she can succeed in completing her love for the organ by extending it to the bearer of the organ" (Ibid., p. 76). Obviously Freud means not the father but the substitute for the father: the woman's potential husband.

183 Sigmund Freud, *Collected Works, Standard Edition*, Volume 15, p. 210.

184 Ibid., Volume 15, p. 210.

185 Webster, *Why Freud Was Wrong*, p. 321.

186 Ibid., p. 319.

Freud believed that man was tragically afflicted by guilt and mental disease, but there was a remedy: Freudian psychoanalysis. His diagnosis of the human situation was essentially the same as Augustine's—although humanity was tainted not so much by sin as by psychopathology. His solution was not sacraments administered by priests within the Church, but sacraments—the psychoanalytical confessional rite—administered by officially accredited psychoanalysts.[187]

The Psychoanalytic Elect

Freud made a distinction between an elect that was suitable for analysis and the rest of humanity that was beyond redemption—helplessly afflicted by neurosis, or even more malignant mental disorders. Although Freud professed to be making merely "objective" and "scientific" discriminations, his language revealed the morally evaluative nature of his distinctions. He wrote in a letter that he found it "gratifying that precisely the most valuable and most highly-developed persons are best suited" for analysis.[188] The elect were evidently those from middle or upper classes—as Freud wrote, "Those patients who do not possess a reasonable degree of education and a fairly

187 At other times Freud was less sanguine about the ability of psychoanalysis to effect universal redemption. In a letter he wrote in 1903, he stated that "deep rooted manifestations of character, traits of an actually degenerate constitution, show themselves as sources of a resistance [to psychoanalysis] that can scarcely be overcome...the constitution of the patient sets a general limit to the curative effects of psychotherapy." Cited in Paul Roazen, *Freud and His Followers* (New York: Knopf, 1975), p. 146.
188 Ibid., p. 148.

reliable character should be refused."[189]

Freud distinguished between the neurotic patient who suffered from an Oedipal complex and more "seriously disturbed" clients suffering from schizophrenia or paranoia. These individuals were, in his view, incurably diseased. Freud wrote, "We must renounce the idea of trying our plan of cure upon psychotics—renounce it perhaps forever or perhaps only for the time being...."[190]

Freud's followers naturally followed his lead. They closed their doors to the "seriously mentally ill" and deemed them incapable of undertaking the kind of psychoanalytic work necessary for correcting their psychopathology. Educated "neurotics" willing to frankly acknowledge their own pathology, to accept their analyst's authority, and to welcome his interpretations were highly regarded in psychoanalytic circles. Psychoanalysts in private practice generally restricted their clientele to this elite class—as they do today.

Thus psychoanalysts were the redeemed intellectual elect, justified and sanctified (all psychoanalysts had themselves undergone psychoanalysis), administering the rites of salvation to the as yet unredeemed elect. Roazen wrote that for Freud a successful analysis constituted a kind of moral medal: "Those who could be helped by psychoanalysis were the people who were really significant."[191]

189 Ibid., p. 148.

190 Furthermore, there were many individuals who had character traits that made them resistant to analysis who also were among the class that nature had consigned to a state of lifelong mental illness. (Analysis ostensibly requires the ability and willingness to temporarily regress to a childlike state.)

191 Paul Roazen, *Freud and His Followers* (New York: Knopf, 1975), p. 146.

CHAPTER FIVE

The Infant's Garden of Eden

When novelist Romain Roland wrote to Freud of his mystical experiences of transcending his ego and of feeling at one with all of creation, Freud acknowledged that such a state can be experienced as blissful but described it as a regression to a "primitive" state normal to infancy. These states were dangerous and based on illusions that adults must transcend. Nonetheless, in Freud's theory the pre-Oedipal child was free from the guilt, the shame, the "neurotic symptoms" that would plague him forever after. The Christian Freudian R.S. Lee wrote in 1948, "Thus every man carries about with him the unconscious memory of a time when he was free from the sense of guilt."[192]

It is relevant to note here that virtually all of the neo-psychoanalysts (Freud's contemporary followers) acknowledge this aboriginal state of bliss. As prominent psychoanalyst Harry Guntripp put it, "Some deep, buried memory of the bliss of life in the womb must lie behind all Garden of Eden fantasies of perfect love-relations, all wistful longings for some mystic unfathomable 'absolute good' which men have experienced in all ages, and all longings for the Golden Age which is always in the past. Its loss must condition what may be called either futile restless dissatisfaction or else the divine discontent which has always plagued human beings."[193]

192   R.S. Lee, *Freud and Christianity* (London: James Clark, 1948), p. 160.
193   Harry Guntripp, *Personality Structure in Human Interaction* (New York: International Universities Press, 1961), p. 361.

Redemption

Since Freud felt the price of civilization was renunciation, it is not surprising that the goals of individual psychoanalysis were rather limited when judged by the standards of a vaster vision—for example, the original Judeo-Christian vision of a Kingdom of God on earth.

"Mental health" meant acceptance of and adjustment to the world as it is. Any other attitude was a product of a regression to infantile primitive modes of thinking. Given the irreconcilable antagonism between self and the world, the desire for happiness was itself pathological, "grandiose." Freud told a patient that psychoanalysis could not make him happy, but "you will be able to convince yourself that much will be gained if we succeed in transforming your hysterical misery into common unhappiness."[194]

Accordingly, the salvific quality of Freud's rhetoric was not derived primarily from the prospect that the individual's degree of unhappiness would be lessened, but rather that his pathology would be cured—perhaps *remission* would be a more accurate term, since Freud assumed that scars would remain and there was always the possibility of a relapse (which is why Freud suggested that the individual should return for analysis every five years).[195] Cure or remission, the ontological deficiency is overcome or ameliorated: thus there is a restoration (at least partial) of the individual's ontological worth that had been severely diminished by infantile pathology. As Roazen

194 Cited in Philip Rieff, *The Mind of the Moralist* (New York: Viking Press, 1959), p. 327.

195 Jeffrey Masson, *Final Analysis* (New York: Addison Wesley, 1990), p. 148.

noted, "To some extent the neurotic patient was a pioneer of a new standard of ethics, in that he had proven worthy of being healed by analysis."[196] To those burdened by a sense or worthlessness, this promise of a restoration of status had a redemptive significance similar to that of Augustinian Christianity. Unfortunately, in both instances the promise was restricted to an elite few.

196   Roazen, *Freud and His Followers*, p. 136.

CHAPTER 6

Freud's Theory of Human Depravity

Although the idea that human beings are evil is explicit in Freud's work, the idea that they are worthless is disguised in medical language. Since most individuals have been indoctrinated to believe that describing someone as severely mentally ill is an objective scientific description rather than an evaluation of worth, it is relevant to cite a couple of examples from Freud's non-clinical writings to corroborate our argument that Freud was thoroughly misanthropic.

The contention that mental illness denotes a state of deficiency is supported by the revelations contained in Freud's private correspondence about his low estimate of human beings' worth—with the exception of the elite that were deserving of Freud's company. He wrote to Lou-Andreas Salomé: "In the depths of my heart I can't help being convinced that my dear fellow men, with a few exceptions, are worthless."[197] At another time he wrote: "The unworthiness of human beings, even of analysts, has always made a deep impression on me...."[198] Elsewhere he confided, "Only a few patients are worth the trouble we spend on them."[199] In another letter he disclosed: "I have found little that is 'good' about human beings as a whole. In my opinion most of them are trash."[200]

197 Roazen, *Freud and His Followers*, p. 146.
198 Cited in Ibid., p. 146.
199 Ibid., p. 146.
200 Ibid., p. 146.

CHAPTER SIX

In a letter to Ludwig Binswanger toward the end of his life, Freud wrote, using the house of science as his metaphor: "I have always lived on the ground floor and in the basement of the building—you maintain that on changing one's viewpoint one can also see an upper floor housing such distinguished guests as religion, art, and others....In this respect you are the conservative, I the revolutionary. If I had another life of work ahead of me, I would dare to offer even those high-born people a home in my lowly hut. I've already found one for religion when I stumbled on the category 'neurosis of mankind.'"[201] Szasz' commentary is pithy. Distinguishing between the "base rhetorician" as opposed to a "noble rhetorician," he writes: "Freud's meaning could not be clearer. His life work, he says, has been devoted to lowering religion from the 'upper floor' into the 'basement'—that is, from inspiration to insanity. If he only had more time left in his life—says the base-rhetorician posing as a scientific revolutionary—he would similarly degrade art and the other lofty accomplishment of the human spirit."[202]

Freudian Fraud

Freud's bizarre theory gained more and more adherents. Artists, intellectuals, philosophers all rallied around Freud as if he was the Messiah that secular man had been yearning for. Despite the exposés of Freud, he still enjoys a virtually godlike status among intellectuals, and among secular Jews. His theories in modified form transformed

228 Cited in Thomas Szasz, *The Myth of Psychotherapy* (New York: Doubleday, 1978), p. 136.
229 Ibid., p. 136-7.

psychology departments in universities around the country. He provided new intellectual glamour for mental health professionals, transforming them from social control agents in mental hospitals to saviors of the soul in private practice. It might be argued that by the middle of the 20th century his religion had almost as many zealous disciples in the United States as Christianity. His theory that infantile trauma was at the root of all adult problems had completely captivated popular culture, despite its lack of any empirical validation.

For Freud the defining dogma of psychoanalysis was the Oedipal complex, which he regarded not only as the source of adult neurosis, but religion, morals, society, and art.[203] And yet the Oedipal complex is sheer invention.[204] It is a matter of common sense that children often feel sexual desires for their parents, but there is no evidence that the boy's sexual feelings toward his mother are strongest between ages three and five, or that they take the form of a desire for coitus. Nor is there any evidence of murderous feelings toward his father. The whole idea of reducing the mother-son relationship to purely biological dimensions runs counter to all available evidence. The idea that the mother remains the paramount love object in the individual life is vitiated by examining the history of romantic love in the last few centuries. (Of course Freud would undoubtedly attempt to interpret this as a manifestation of transference.)

Furthermore, the article of faith that has become the mainstay of popular culture—that an adult's life is deter-

203 See Jerome Neu, ed., *The Cambridge Companion to Freud* (Cambridge: Cambridge University Press, 1991).
204 Webster, *Why Freud Was Wrong*, pp. 254-258.

mined entirely by events in the first five years of life—has been definitively disproved. Events during these years have been shown to have no predictive validity in relation to behavior shown during adulthood.[205]

Freud's success in imposing his narrative on modern culture is astonishing, but no more astonishing than the success of Augustine, Calvin, and Luther in other eras. The tragedy is that the original Christian vision has been eclipsed and that the religious strivings of human beings were colonized by these movements that reified the status quo and suppressed the sense of God-given possibility aroused by Jesus, and which has surfaced at rare moments time and time again in the historical life of humanity.

Freud's own case studies—he wrote only four—are paradigmatic of the way a person's life story can be twisted and distorted so that it conforms to the narrative entrenched in the mind of the authority. The case of Dora analyzed by Freud has been subjected to scrutiny by Roy Porter[206] and Jeffrey Masson,[207] who come to similar conclusions. Dora, as a fourteen-year-old, was sexually approached in a manner that would be regarded as "abusive" today, considering her age and the fact that her attempted seducer was a married friend of her father, "Herr K." Her father, in effect, sanctioned his friend's advances

205   See Seth Farber, "Institutional Mental Health and Social Control: The Ravages of Epistemological Hubris," *The Journal of Mind and Behavior*, Special Issue, Volume 11, Numbers 3 and 4, 1990.

206   Roy Porter, *A Social History of Madness* (New York: Weidenfeld and Nicolson, 1987).

207   Jeffrey Masson, *Against Therapy* (New York: MacMillan, 1988).

to his daughter [to Dora] because he himself was having an affair with Herr K's wife. By the standards of the time it was undoubtedly "improper" behavior, and yet Dora's own disturbance over this and similar incidents was entirely dismissed by Freud.[208] In reality, Freud told Dora she was repressing her sexual love for Herr K; it was this that caused her "mental illness," her depression, her nervous cough, and her migraine headaches. The reason she could not acknowledge her love for Herr K was because she had an Oedipal fixation on her father.

Freud's theories demanded that he ignore the actual events in individuals' present lives that caused them to respond emotionally and sometimes traumatically. Thus he interpreted these responses as "symptoms" of pathological processes initiated in the past. He invariably denied the goal-directed nature of his patients' actions and presented them as symptoms beyond their control. As Freud was oblivious to quite plausible simpler explanations of why his patients were unhappy, he substituted instead his own fantastic constructions.

There were enough disturbing events in Dora's present life and in her recent past when Freud met her—including Freud's own attempts to invalidate her perceptions and feelings and persuade her that she was mentally disordered—to explain her trauma without having to invoke events in her early childhood. Masson wrote about Dora, "She felt conspired against. She *was* conspired against. She felt lied to. She *was* lied to. She felt used. She *was* used. She was beginning to lose her faith in justice, in

208 Masson, *Against Therapy*, pp. 113-118, and Porter, *A Social History of Madness*, pp. 52-58.

integrity—in short, the world. She was right."[209] She had hoped that Freud would understand her feelings—he dismissed them as symptoms of pathology. Unlike most of his other patients who accepted the great man's interpretations at the expense of their own intuitions and self-respect, she bolted, quitting psychoanalysis.

Freud's Neo-Augustinianism

In 1960, Szasz attempted to bring to the attention of the public the idea that mental illness is a metaphor, and a metaphor that he believed was degrading and obfuscating. Szasz did not explicate all the theological implications of this metaphor. The term *mental disorder, mental illness*, or *psychopathology* presupposes the concept of mental order. The former is necessarily relative to the latter. When Freud claimed that his patients were suffering from mental disorders, he must have assumed, consciously or unconsciously, the concept of mental order—obviously not an order ordained by God, as Freud was an atheist.

In medicine there is a near consensus (until recently at least) about what is natural, what is in order. An illness is a breach of the order of nature. As a physician, Freud assumed that there was an order of nature—of unquestionable authority—governing the body. Freud tacitly extended the sovereignty of nature's order to psychological life.

For Freud, Nature had replaced God as the ultimate source of authority. Although he claimed to be a scientist who eschewed value judgments, he assumed that what was in accord with Nature had positive value, and what

209   Ibid., p. 61 (emphasis added).

was unnatural had negative value. To assert that an individual suffers from neurosis, from psychopathology, from mental illness, from disease, is to posit necessarily the existence of a natural order that has been violated or breached in some manner such that its reign has been undermined or destroyed. Unlike a violation of the order of God, a breach of the order of Nature necessarily means that the organism has been subjected to either a disease or an injury. In either case the inner being of the individual is transformed: either infected with disease, or injured. The pretense that this assertion is merely a scientific description, not an evaluation, is hollow. Since the mind, by definition, is an immaterial entity that cannot be literally diseased or damaged, this metaphor has a univocal meaning: There has been a vitiation or diminution of the individual's worth.

The only question is, to what degree? While repudiating the existence of God, Freud has arrived at a philosophical position almost identical to Augustine's, albeit less severe. Augustine stated that human beings' souls were dead. Freud stated that they were diseased, in most instances irreparably so. In either case, there is something fundamentally wrong. Man is essentially flawed. Being is deficient.

But there is a major problem in the inner coherence of Freud's theory. On the one hand, he tells us that human beings are mentally ill as a result of experiencing the Oedipal complex. On the other hand, he tells us that everyone, or almost everyone, experiences a "neurotic phase in the course of their development"[210] arising from Oedipal

210 Cited in Reuben Fine, *The History of Psychoanalysis* (Northvale, New Jersey: n.d.), p. 70.

conflicts. This clearly implies that this phase—however uncomfortable or painful—is natural, and therefore not "neurotic." (The idea that suffering is ipso facto pathological is absurd, as can be easily seen when one considers the phenomenon of pregnancy and childbirth.) Freud implies that neurosis is both universal and inevitable. In fact, his own theories and case histories unfold with the same quality of preordained fate that one finds in *Oedipus Rex* and other tragedies. If Freud is correct, then on what possible basis could he stake his claim that the Oedipal complex is the cause of psychopathology, i.e., of a breach in the order of nature?

It is true that Freud paints a relatively roseate picture of the phase in the child's life before the Oedipal stage. However, two points must be kept in mind. In the first place, the child is destined, as it were, to undergo the Oedipal complex—as a *developmental phase*. To put this in other terms, one could say that it is preordained, willed by Nature. But where, then, is that beneficent, human-friendly Nature that the very concept of psychopathology implies has been breached or violated—and would have retained its benevolent reign over humanity had not illness or injury occurred? In the second place, in Freud's theory, there is no beneficent nature from the beginning since even the newborn infant is "evil" and harbors the seeds of the depraved desires that manifest themselves later. For Freud there is no natural state of happiness and innocence that is breached by disease; there is merely a state of infant bliss, whose ephemeral existence is no more natural (or less) than its disappearance.

Undoubtedly these reflections may strike many readers as surprising. This is because they have identified

Freudianism with what Freudianism became—after Freud. This is the theory, the dogma lodged securely in the popular imagination, that all adult problems result from inadequate (or malicious) parenting during the first few years of a child's life. It is this dogma that is incorporated in virtually all Freudian theories today, and that brings Freudianism closer to Augustinianism: The suffering of humanity is accidental, not ordained by God (or by Nature as the Freudians put it) but results from man's own sinful deeds. In the revised Freudian version of original sin, bad parents have replaced bad Adam. But both accounts decree that man is responsible for this tragic denouement—not God, not Nature.

Freud's theory was inconsistent: According to him, the Oedipal phase was natural. But it produced baneful consequences that were unnatural, i.e., pathological. This is the contradiction at the heart of Freud's theory: a natural process that engenders pathological phenomena. Without acknowledging the weakness in Freud's theory, his followers corrected it by accounting for the frequently destructive putative consequences of the Oedipal phase by positing a breach in the natural order caused by parental inadequacy, egocentricity and/or abusiveness. In other words, Freud's disciples believe that the results of the Oedipal phase (and other childhood phases) in theory could be (in practice almost never were) completely natural upon one essential condition: that the parents act "maturely," thereby assisting, as it were, the natural developmental process. (This premise, stated or unstated, informs virtually all of the Freudian theories and case studies that are done today.) If parents acted in a mature manner, the Freudians imply, their children would become mentally healthy, happy, well-adjusted adults. It is assumed that this almost never occurs. The typical scenario is that parental misdeeds cause children to be thrust outside the benevolent order of nature, and to become afflicted by psychopathology. This doctrine, which is considered to be the quintessence of Freudian psychoanalytic theory, was not proposed by Freud himself. Early in his career Freud had developed a theory like this, as Jeffrey Masson shows, but abandoned it when he discovered it displeased his fellow physicians.

Besides Freud's desire for professional acceptance, there is another reason he may have avoided making this move. Perhaps he found it as difficult to posit a benevolent Nature, as he did a beneficent God. He remained transfixed throughout his life by poor Oedipus, whose fate was preordained before he was born. The parallel with Calvin, who believed that God ordained Adam's fall, is striking.

But no sooner had Freud declared Nature to be responsible for the tragic Oedipal complex, than he felt compelled to call a truce. Freud maintained unwaveringly that man suffered from psychopathology. As a physician, in order to maintain his reputation for competence, he had no choice but to claim that he could cure individuals of their pathology, i.e., bring them back under the sovereignty of Nature's beneficent reign. Theoretically, Freud could maintain that man and nature were permanently at odds—which he often came close to doing (and actually did at times)—but where would that have left Freud, an atheist with Messianic aspirations? It was far more expedient to promise a reconciliation between Nature and humanity—and to ignore Nature's alleged responsibility for the Oedipal complex that had tragically blighted the life of individuals for centuries. After all, this was a grand opportunity for psychoanalysis—Freud did not hesitate to nominate his Science of Psychoanalysis as the most worthy candidate (the only worthy candidate) for overcoming this breach of nature: of effecting at least a partial reconciliation, and thus a partial restoration of the individual's worth. On the other hand, Freud viewed all of his former collaborators who disagreed with him and formed their own schools of therapy as traitors to the great cause.

Freudian theory manifests the salient features of Augustinism delineated above: First, the person is flawed, spiritually defective, as a result of infantile traumas. Free will is almost entirely eliminated. Virtually all of the patient's actions become involuntary symptomatic manifestations of pathological processes. There is no salvation outside of psychoanalysis—and only for the elect.

The second condition is only partially met in Freudian theory. There is not an intention of Nature that is thwarted by human action. (In psychoanalysis today, as noted above, this condition is met by positing that "toxic parents" unwittingly or maliciously inflict emotional damage on their young children.) Nevertheless, there is a paradisical state that exists in the beginning for which human beings harbor an eternal nostalgia—the early infant relationship with the mother.

Third, humanity is divided into two groups—an elect susceptible to psychoanalysis, and the reprobate who cannot be cured.

Fourth, there is no transcendent God. Nevertheless, there is by implication a transcendent Nature—possessing absolute ethical and ontological sanction—with whom the individual can never be fully reconciled but with whom the elect can be partially reconciled through the modality of Freudian psychoanalysis.

Fifth, there is the Augustinian preoccupation with individual guilt and unworthiness; and sixth, Freud does not advocate any kind of collective social reform but is enthralled by the vision of an individualistic salvation—partial sanctification through the modality of psychoanalysis.

The Secular Priesthood

The question imposes itself: How can one reconcile Freud's postulate of a natural order (entailed as we saw by the idea of psychopathology)—which by virtue of it being natural possesses absolute ontological and ethical sanction—with the positivist pretensions of psychoanalysis to be an "objective science" that eschews value judgments? Clearly one cannot.

Freud had two alternative approaches he could have taken to more effectively fortify himself from the charge of being termed evaluative: one honest, the other dishonest. He could have described his patients as suffering individuals contending with the problems of life in a difficult world. He did not need to ascribe pathology to them. This was undoubtedly the way Freud tended to see himself, for the most part.[211] The concept of psychopathology, of ontological deficiency, was entirely gratuitous. Freud, for example, could have sympathized with Dora's plight, could even have seen her as a courageous young woman

---

211 Although he also saw himself as a kind of secular Messiah, singled out by destiny to play a grand role in the course of modern history. See Porter, *A Social History of Madness*, pp. 216-228.

contending as best she could with the hypocrisy, blatant insensitivity, and selfishness of the adults in her world. Freud did not need to invent a profound neurosis to explain her behavior and emotions. The same could be demonstrated for Freud's other patients, as Jeffrey Masson and Roy Porter have shown. Freud could even have reconciled a non-pathological model with the existence of "Oedipal conflicts," although he would have had to acknowledge that his patients were facing difficult circumstances in their present lives, instead of seeing Oedipus lurking around every corner.

Alternatively, Freud could have postulated that manifestations of mental anguish are actually symptoms of physical illnesses, brain diseases, or genetic flaws. In this way, he could have disguised more effectively the value-laden nature of his enterprise. Freud flirted with this theory but finally took the psychological route, transfixed as he was with infantile sexuality and the Oedipal complex. The biological approach was the route that the mental health professions took in the late 1970s and 1980s (partially as a result of a massive influx of dollars from the manufacturers of psychiatric drugs) in a last-ditch effort to salvage the idea that society is inevitably comprised of winners and losers, of the fit and the unfit in the Darwinian social jungle, of the elect and the reprobate, and that it is Nature that determines individuals' fate in advance before they are born.

Freud's positivist pretensions cannot withstand postmodernist scrutiny. Ironically, although he thought that he had uncovered the neurotic basis of religion—an infantile yearning for an external source of authority that would endow the individual's life with value—Freud himself had the same need. He was a crypto-theist. He called this authority "nature," and he deemed the violation of its commandments as pathology. As a Christian, I believe that Freud's religious needs merely corroborate the contention that the desire for God is a constituent element of our being as creatures.

Freudian Epistemological Hubris

At this point a final epistemological question arises: How did Freud know? How did he and his epigones know what is "natural" and what is "pathological?" As a Christian, I believe that God has revealed Himself in Christ—and that this is the source of the norms I hold binding. Although Freud held himself in high esteem, as an atheist he could not very well claim to have had a special divine revelation. Instead, he asserted—and his followers concurred—that his unique scientific genius had led him to the discoveries he had made and that his own case studies and self-psychoanalysis corroborated his theories.

In actuality, the order of nature and its norms was Freud's own construction. But in this way Freud was not different from the Augustinian priesthood that had ruled society for centuries when human beings worshipped God rather than Science. Freud's predecessors claimed that their religious authority and credentials enabled them to know God's will, and thus to discern the signs of heresy and witchcraft. Freud evidently intended that the power to define what was natural and what was pathological be passed on to his loyal disciples throughout history, in a kind of apostolic succession. However, the guilds of the mental health professions refused to cede this privilege entirely and only to Freud's disciples. While they basked for decades in the intellectual prestige psychoanalysis had bestowed upon them, they refused to grant hegemony to any one school of psychology but arrogated to themselves as a group the right to determine what is natural, and what is pathological. The kinds and degrees of mental illnesses, of "deficiency" as a human being, are described and codified in *The Diagnostic and Statistical Manual of Mental Disorders*, first published in 1952, which remains the Bible of the mental health professions.

CHAPTER 7

Neo-Freudianism in the Modern Era

Despite the development in the last few decades of a plethora of approaches to therapy, rumors of the death of Freudianism (particularly in its neo-Freudian variance) have been greatly exaggerated, to paraphrase Mark Twain. While the biological model provides a rationale for the administration of psychiatric drugs, i.e., medication, and thus is dominant within the public mental health field, it has by no means replaced the psychoanalytic model, i.e., the revisionist Freudian model. In most mental health centers the models coexist peacefully: The psychiatrist dispenses drugs (and, depending on his orientation, sometimes also does therapy), and other mental health professionals engage patients in psychotherapy, almost always based on a psychoanalytic model.

It is psychoanalytic theory—which I will here refer to as neo-Freudianism—that continues as the structure that undergirds the mental health mission.[212] For this reason it is Freudian and neo-Freudian theories that are taught, and endorsed as the most "scientific humanistic" approach to the mind, in most graduate programs in psychology and

212 In other words, I will break with the custom that restricts the term "neo-Freudian" to a few Freudian theorists, mostly prominently Erich Fromm, Karen Horney and Clara Thompson. I will use the term *neo-Freudian* to refer to modern psychoanalytic thought in general, in order to avoid minimizing the latter's historical and ideological commitments, which are evidenced both by the reverence with which Freud is regarded by this school, and the influence that his work has had upon their own theories.

in social work, as well as in most advanced undergraduate courses in psychology. It is neo-Freudianism that satisfies in the modern world, as will be shown, the religious needs of mental health professionals and their patients, and at the same time serves to disguise the theological nature of the mental health mission. At the same time, it is undeniable that the influence of neo-Freudianism has been severely curtailed and its hegemony undermined by the meteoric displays of biological psychiatry.

The Era of Freud

The popularity of Freudian theory burgeoned after World War II. E. Fuller Torrey's lively chronicle[213] discussed the factors that facilitated the gradual development of a Freudian popular culture in the United States after the war. On the one hand, the rise and defeat of Nazism undermined the popularity of the hereditarian and racist anthropologies that had been popular in American academic circles in the 1920s and 1930, and diffused through popular culture by racist tracts. On the other hand, the development of the Cold War in the 1940s and 1950s and the domestic persecution of Communists, leftists, and liberal "fellow travellers" made Freudianism a more attractive channel for the creative energies of dissatisfied intellectuals than Marxism—this was in contrast to the early 1930s, where virtually all independent intellectuals gravitated to one brand of Marxism or another. These intellectuals were catalysts in the dissemination of Freudian dogmas during the 1950s and 1960s.

213 E. Fuller Torrey, *Freudian Fraud* (New York: Harper Collins, 1992).

In 1956 Alfred Kazin stated in *The New York Times* magazine that Freud's importance for understanding nature was comparable to Copernicus, Darwin, and Einstein. He implied that we were now living in the era of Freud. As noted above, the Freudianism that was incorporated into American culture was revisionist and based on the doctrine that the primary cause of adult pathology was inadequate parenting.

Benjamin Spock, whose book *Baby and Child Care* sold over forty million copies, propagated a watered-down Freudian faith through his books and magazine articles in the 1950s. Spock demonstrated his Freudian pedigree by his repeated warning to parents to be particularly patient with children during the crucial Oedipal phase. Spock never hesitated to recommend psychoanalytic psychotherapy for virtually any persistent behavioral anomaly that a child manifested.

In 1963, John Kennedy signed into law a bill that created federally funded community mental health centers around the country. Dr. Robert Felix, director of the National Institute of Mental Health, established in 1946, urged his colleagues to take advantage of the new legislation and to work to ensure that mental health services would be "fully integrated into and a regular and continuing part of the total social environment."[214] The number of mental health professionals began growing exponentially after World War II. In 1943 there were 9,000 psychiatrists, psychologists, and social workers. In 1992 there were 200,000: 40,000 psychiatrists, 70,000 psychologists, and 80,000 psychiatric social workers—a twenty-two-fold increase during the years in which the national population did not quite

214 Ibid., p. 193.

double. All of the professionals were indoctrinated with Freudian theories in graduate school—in 1970, Freudianism had such an intellectual allure that an estimated one-third of all psychiatrists had undertaken expensive postgraduate psychoanalytic training.[215]

Ten million Americans consult psychiatrists, psychologists, or social workers today, and millions more consult marriage counselors, family therapists, pastoral counselors, and the like. The common denominator of virtually all of these forms of therapies until the 1980s was the neo-Freudian assumption that all adult intrapersonal and interpersonal problems originate in inadequate parenting in the first few years of life. As Kenneth Gergen, professor of psychology at Swarthmore College, observed in 1977, contemporary culture has "almost fully accepted the assumption that early experience is vital in shaping adult behavior."[216] Or as Torrey put it, "Freud's theory has been incorporated into the very soul of the nation."[217]

Neo-Freudian Ego Psychology

There was no question in my own mind by the time I had completed my Masters Degree in Psychology in 1978 that neo-Freudian theory and therapy was the means for the redemption of humanity. My only heresy (as stated above) was that I believed that even schizophrenics (ac-

215 Webster, *Why Freud Was Wrong* (New York: Basic Books, 1995).

216 Cited in Seth Farber, Ph.D., "Institutional Mental Health and Social Control," in David Cohen, ed., *Challenging the Therapeutic State*, Special Issue of *The Journal of Mind and Behavior*, Vol. II, Nos. 3-4, p. 289.

217 Torrey, *Freudian Fraud*, p. 213.

cording to Freudianism, the most "severely mentally ill") could be saved. That is, I refused to accept the conventional Freudian wisdom which divided the population into (1) a small elect who was worthy of true psychoanalysis, (2) a larger number of "borderline" cases who could be helped to function better through psychotherapy, and (3) a sizable minority of psychotics who were irreparably damaged.

The neo-Freudian theories that were and still are taught in graduate schools I attended in the late 1970s and early 1980s were termed "ego psychology," "object-relations," and "self psychology." All of these theories posited that Freud had erred by placing the locus of pathology in the Oedipal phase. The most serious pathologies originated in the "oral" phase—when the child related to his mother through the modality of his mouth: the greater the trauma, the more severe the adult pathology. Pathology resulted either in excessive emotional dependency upon others or in a schizoid withdrawal from others. The latter, according to neo-Freudianism, was really a disguised manifestation of the former, since the intensity of the individual's dependency needs led him to repress them and to attempt to "compensate" for them through various pathological symptoms.

The greatest danger that the individual faced is that the ego, i.e., that facet of the psyche that was responsible for recognizing and coping with "reality," would emerge from the oral phase too weak and impaired to undergo psychoanalysis that required a reliving of the early infantile trauma. The fortunate person had an ego strong enough to undergo psychoanalysis, and could expect a partial or total cure after several years of intensive psychoanalytic "work." If the ego was impaired, psychoanalysis was contraindicated as it might lead to the breakdown of the ego during the process of reliving the early infantile trauma. This would result in psychosis, which entailed the spectre of permanent regression to a primitive, i.e., infantile, state of functioning. In borderline cases with weak egos, the therapeutic task was to leave the "core of the pathology" untouched, and to concentrate on strengthening the ego so that the individual could function adequately despite the chronic psychopathology that would prevent him from ever experiencing the full depth of intimacy and creativity available to the successfully psychoanalyzed patient.

A highly acclaimed neo-Freudian textbook published in 1974[218] that received plaudits from the most highly esteemed modern Freudian theorists codified the distinctions made above. Psychoanalytically oriented psychotherapy "takes the unconscious very much into account and has structural change as its optimal goal."[219] Such "far-reaching personality change" takes longer than mere "behavioral change."[220] This non sequitur of a "far-reaching personality change" that cannot be assessed by behavioral changes is a typical psychoanalytic ploy. Obviously, the authors are implying that only trained and properly certified psychoanalysts (like themselves) have the capacity to intuit or discern when profound changes (invisible to the unpsychoanalytic eye) occurs, and consequently only they can pronounce that the patient is cured of his or her ontological deficiency.

218 Gertrude and Rubin Blanck, *Ego Psychology Theory and Practice, Volumes I and II* (New York: Columbia University Press, 1974).
219 Ibid., Volume I, p. 3.
220 Ibid., p. 3.

At any rate, psychoanalytically oriented therapy as opposed to mere psychotherapy derived from psychoanalytic theory is, according to the authors, both more ambitious and more exclusive. It should not be undertaken with either psychotic or "borderline" personalities, both of whom are more psychologically impaired than "neurotics." The authors comment, "Borderline structures have potential for irreversible, or, at best, difficult-to-reverse regression...."[221]

The authors go on to remind us of the precedent set by the Ultimate Authority: "We remind ourselves here that Freud even recommended a trial analysis after which the patient was to be dismissed if it was found that his ego was not capable of enduring it."[222] The authors do not mention that the determination that this patient's ego is too weak is made exclusively by the analyst, and often upon completely arbitrary grounds—e.g., if the "patient" did not agree with the analyst's interpretation, as Dora did not agree with Freud's. (Dora of course left Freud before he took the opportunity to "dismiss" her.)

The Blancks' textbook is written to help professionals do psychotherapy with those borderline cases who are not capable of undergoing full-blown psychoanalysis. The psychotherapist is advised not to develop high expectations for their clients, since mere psychotherapy can never be as effective as "the technique of psychoanalysis."[223] They

221   Ibid., p. 131.
222   Ibid., p. 8.
223   Ibid., p. 10.

warn their readers to realize that their goals as psychotherapists are limited to "healing the damaged ego" of the borderline personality without addressing the pathology which lies "deeper" in the psyche than the ego. Furthermore, for psychotics even this may be too much to accomplish, as the authors note that "the most severe pathologies are essentially irreversible."[224] However, readers are reassured: "This does not at all mean that maintaining the patient at whatever may be his optimal level of functioning is not worthwhile."[225]

Thus the Blancks' textbook clearly exemplifies two salient characteristics of neo-Freudianism. In the first place, individuals are assigned to discreet categories that supposedly reveal not only the essential condition of their psyche, i.e., their "diagnosis," but also whatever changes may or may not be expected of them, i.e., their "prognosis." These expectations that are conveyed to their readers, apprentice psychotherapists, act inevitably as self-fulfilling prophecies. Second, neo-Freudians regard those patients who are not capable of proper psychoanalysis with a mixture of condescension, pity, and disdain.

For the neo-Freudian, psychoanalysis is the sacrament that initiates the qualified patient into the psychoanalytic elect, and the authors confess their faith in the sole efficacy of this sacrament. "We do not expect in the long run, that greater theoretical knowledge and improved techniques will ever bring psychotherapy to as favorable a prognostic position as psychoanalysis."[226]

---

224 Ibid., p. 10.
225 Ibid., p. 10 (emphasis added).
226 Ibid., p. 10.

CHAPTER SEVEN

A statement that rules out any further progress in the field of psychotherapy is made purely on a priori grounds—this strikingly exemplifies the dogmatism of the neo-Freudians. In actuality, a number of studies have demonstrated that psychoanalysis is no more effective than other forms of therapy. (Some have indicated that it is less effective.) Of course the Blancks would undoubtedly dismiss the conclusion of the research since it was based on an assessment of "mere behavioral change" as opposed to the "far-reaching personality change" that they assure us is the goal of psychoanalytic therapy.

Obviously the implication of this a priori argument is that those who are not capable of analysis can never expect a "more favorable prognosis," i.e., to be cured.

Essentially we have here a five-tiered caste system. There are three tiers among the unredeemed: (1) at the bottom schizophrenics and other psychotics, who are not, and will never be, capable of undergoing psychoanalysis, and who only can be maintained by psychotherapy at the highest level of functioning they are able to reach; (2) borderline personalities, whose egos can be "built up" by psychotherapy; some of this class may qualify for psychoanalysis after years of psychotherapy; and (3) "neurotics," who comprise the majority of the elect who are fit to undergo the rigors of psychoanalysis. Among the redeemed are: (4) successfully psychoanalyzed patients; and (5) the psychoanalysts themselves, who by virtue of their professional status, their mastery of the Freudian esoteric theory, and their initiation into the Freudian cult possess the status that elevates them (at least in their own minds) above even the most socially and financially successful individuals.

Blanck and Blanck articulate the consensus that dominated the mental health field during the time in which I was studying and practicing psychoanalytically derived psychotherapy in the late 1970s and early 1980s. From my discussion with mental health professionals, it is still extant today, although it is qualified by some of the considerations introduced by biological psychiatry. In one Blanck were not typical of most mental health professionals. Many mental health professionals (including many psychoanalysts during that time) believed that "psychosis" was caused not by inadequate parenting during the early phase of development but by genetic or biological defects. This view is dominant in the mental health professions today.

The Neo-Freudian Tragedy

The neo-Freudians have corrected the internal inconsistency in Freud's theory; they can now coherently account for their attribution of pathology. The infant is born under the benevolent sovereignty of nature. But the natural process of development is disturbed by parents who are too egocentric to minister to their children's needs in a natural manner, so to speak. Thus nature is disturbed, and pathological processes assume control of the individual's psyche, which undergoes a rupture of its original unity under the impact of trauma.

But while this narrative is coherent, it remains problematic. First, there was not a homeostatic order of nature that was disturbed by parental ineptitude. The fetus-infant-child confronts one biological trauma after another, including, most saliently, the process of birth. The infant is in a continuous state of pain and/or discomfort due to his or her extreme vulnerability to the environment. Since physical trauma is a natural part of development, why should we assume that trauma caused by psychological events results in a breach in the order of nature?

The neo-Freudian would probably claim that psychological events are more damaging to the infant than physiological events. But even if we grant that parental inadequacy is more traumatic than physiological ordeals, and thus may in that sense be said to cause a breach in the natural process of development, the epistemological question remains: How do the neo-Freudians know that the scheme they have constructed of "good-enough parenting"[227] was *intended* by Nature (i.e., is in "the natural order of things," to use Guntrip's phrase)? After all, Nature does not reveal her will, her intention, her plan through revelation, as God does.

The construct of psychopathology depends upon an unacknowledged narrative ploy that the Freudians standardly make. A hypothetical ideal (a good enough childhood) is treated as if were a reality (before the infant was traumatized), or as if it was *meant* or intended to have been a reality, *but then* certain senseless events occurred (parental misdeeds of commission and omission) resulting in a disorder, a violation of what was intended by Nature. (Since the neo-Freudians are positivists—i.e., they claim to be making only scientific descriptions, not evaluations — they cannot acknowledge that they have posited an order of nature that possesses absolute value.) The individual whose mind is no longer in accord with the order of nature is *ipso facto* afflicted with psychopathology, he or

227 Winnicott's phrase, cited in Guntrip in Ibid., p. 385.

she is now existentially deficient, lacking in worth, if not altogether worthless.

For the neo-Freudian, the idea of a "natural" childhood free from significant traumas acts as a disguised substitute for the Christian concept of the Garden of Eden before the Fall. The idea that a childhood without significant trauma is natural is completely arbitrary. It is precisely because individuals have goals that they can confront obstacles, and in the process experience frustration and suffering. It is always possible to imagine a more optimal state where the attainment of the goals would entail less suffering and effort. But the fact that such an ideal state does not exist does not imply that something unnatural has taken place. Thus the neo-Freudian account is a narrative construction, not an empirical "scientific" description.

Furthermore, the credibility of the neo-Freudian narrative depends on several contentions that are not supported by research. First, the dogma that psychoanalysis is the only effective treatment is false, as noted above. Second, neo-Freudians believe that anxiety about "object loss" in the first few years of life is the major determinant of adult pathology. But as Kagan noted, "The variation and degree of anxiety over loss of access to attachment figures during the first three years of life predicted no significant behavior in adolescence or adulthood."[228] Third, neo-Freudians contend that their diagnostic categories reflect actual ontological distinctions in human beings. It is implied that the individual's ability to change and grow is severely limited by the time he or she comes to the neo-

228 Cited in Farber, "Institutional Mental Health and Social Control," p. 289.

Freudian for help. But Gergen shows that the data collected by life span developmental researchers indicate that development is idiosyncratic and unpredictable: "The individual seems fundamentally flexible in most aspects of personal functioning. Significant change in the life course may occur at any time...An immense panoply of development forms seems possible; which particular form emerges may depend on a confluence of particulars, the existence of which is fundamentally unsystematic."[229] Thus, the intractability that neo-Freudians find among "the severely mentally ill" is an artifact of their own practices, a self-fulfilling prophecy.

How is it that the narrative structure undergirding neo-Freudian "science" has remained undetected for so many decades despite extensive examination? Why has its ascription of "psychopathology" to the individual been so rarely challenged?

I believe it is because neo-Freudianism is a secularization of the Augustinian version of the narrative of the Fall, the story that has captivated the collective imagination of Western humanity for centuries. It is part of our culture, and thus is as unnoticeable as the air we breathe. Furthermore, it has an irresistible appeal for modern men and women, who feel a strong need for redemption at the same time they have repudiated traditional religions as "unscientific."

Neo-Freudianism as Augustinianism

Neo-Freudianism possesses the six essential characteristics of Augustinianism. First, the person is flawed to a

___

229 Cited in Ibid., p. 289.

greater or lesser degree and lacking in worth. There is a hierarchy of worth determined by neo-Freudians. Free will is circumscribed and, in the case of the "schizophrenic," virtually eliminated. Second, the situation was not what was originally intended. The "bad" deeds of parents leads to a rupture of the state of nature. Third, humanity is divided into an elect, which is qualified to receive the sacrament of psychoanalysis, and those who are not. Those who are not will always be defective, severely mentally ill, incapable (and unworthy, it is implied) of loving fully.

Augustine had emphasized the transcendence of God as compared to the depravity of human beings. For God, neo-Freudianism substitutes Nature. What is natural is good, healthy, whole, but the adult individual is, after suffering the traumas of childhood, in an unnatural state: He is diseased, sick, divided, his ego is impaired, weak, split in warring factions. He is entirely "outside" of the benevolent reign of Nature. The pathology is "deeply rooted," going down into the very foundations of the individual's being. The opposition between nature and man is as radical in neo-Freudianism as is the opposition between God and man in Augustinianism.

Fifth, there is a preoccupation with morbidity, disease, ontological flaw, unworthiness. The sense of sin, however, is entirely or almost entirely eliminated by the neo-Freudians, since the patient is not responsible for his situation but is a victim of his parents' egocentricity. Sixth, this preoccupation with deficiency leads to an individualistic vision of salvation antithetical to the Christian vision of a new social and cosmic order.

The similarities are outstanding, but there is a new element that comes into play in neo-Freudianism: pathos.

This is absent or barely present in classical Augustinianism and muted in classical Freudianism, which as we have seen is closer to Augustinianism. This is because in neo-Freudianism the infant is presented as an innocent victim meriting pity, rather than as in Augustinianism as an evil sinner deserving of no compassion. Thus the neo-Freudian narrative has the appeal of tragedy—the pathos of the fall of the noble hero provides both catharsis and the excitement of entering into the realm of grandeur.

Ironically, neo-Freudianism is inexorably fixated on the past. The tragic strain that runs throughout neo-Freudian or psychoanalytic theory is based on the implicit idea that things were meant to be different, that we were meant to have had a different kind of childhood than the one we actually did have. This idea engenders further ruminations such as, "It did not have to have happened the way it did," or "It could have been different."

Psychoanalysts have been writing a tragic story about the human situation. One cannot read psychoanalytic literature without being overwhelmed by a profound sense of pathos, without being haunted by a sense of "It could have been" and "almost." A mournful tune plays beneath the psychoanalytic lyrics: "It could have been....It could have been....It could have been."

Northrop Frye in his classic text described the hero of the tragic story: The tragic hero has normally had an extraordinary, often a nearly divine destiny almost within his grasp, and the glory of that original vision never quite fades out of tragedy....While catastrophe is a normal end of tragedy, this is balanced by an equally significant original greatness, a paradise lost."[230]

This is the "almost" that haunts the psychoanalytic tale. In Augustinian Christianity, it is typically balanced by the glorious promise of salvation, at least for a few elect, but for the Freudian the redemption offered to the elite groups of neurotics never attains to the grandeur of what might have been achieved. The psychoanalytic hero, of course, is the newborn infant who possesses a whole ego, a psyche of pristine purity and integrity, who has a nearly divine destiny almost within his or her grasp, but whose ego is then irreparably damaged by the very individuals who cherish the greatest hope for the infant child: his or her parents.

Psychoanalytic literature betrays a nostalgia for a past that never was, for a "might have been" that is a figment of the imagination. This, of course, is ironic, because psychoanalysis announced its arrival as a power that had come both to reveal that human beings are fixated on the past and to liberate them from that fixation. It cannot fulfill that aspiration, it cannot forge a trail to a brighter future. It is too burdened by a sense of pathos to realize how brilliantly the promise of the future can shine for humanity, if we have the strength to gaze at it with the naked eyes of hope and faith.

For the psychoanalyst, the vision of what could have been is vivid and resplendent, whereas the vision of what could be is at best tarnished and obscure. For the neo-Freudian the past is far more real than the future. Needless to say, the Christian vision of the Kingdom of Heaven

---

230 Northrop Frye, *Anatomy of Criticism* (Princeton, New Jersey: Princeton University Press, 1973), p. 210.

on earth is regarded as nothing more than a projection of a childhood fantasy.

The impact of neo-Freudianism on American culture (and on Western Europe) can hardly be exaggerated. Its vision of human beings as flawed, mentally diseased, afflicted with psycho-pathology, psychologically disordered—in short, ontologically deficient, lacking in worth to a greater or lesser degree—has pervaded popular culture, instilling in almost everyone who comes under its influence a basic sense of self-doubt. The assumption of the "diagnostic" manual that is used by virtually all mental health professionals is that anyone who experiences suffering in life and seeks some kind of assistance, is *ipso facto* suffering from some kind of "mental disorder." Popular psychology, and popular movements like the variety of twelve-step recovery groups, have uncritically accepted the assumptions of neo-Freudianism that the individual is deficient. The recovery worldview is becoming prevalent in American popular culture.[231]

It is significant that Woody Allen, a world-renowned actor and film auteur, internationally acclaimed and hailed by many intellectuals as a genius, has spent forty

231 See Wendy Kaminer, *I'm Dysfunctional, You're Dysfunctional* (New York: Addison-Wesley, 1992). Some critics focusing on schools of psychology that have been more popular among Christians, such as that of Carl Rogers or Carl Jung, have critiqued them for their overly sanguine view of human nature. See, for example, Paul Vitz, *Psychology as Religion* (Grand Rapids, Michigan: Eerdmans Publishing Company, 1994). I want to note: (1) The neo-Freudian ontology is more prevalent in American culture, and (2) the main problem with these theories is *not* that they are optimistic, but that their optimism is facile, that it has no ontological or theological grounding.

years of his life going to a psychoanalyst daily, presumably hoping to attain a sense of adequacy, of basic worth. Influenced by neo-Freudianism, the aspiring individual views himself as a damaged individual. On the most basic fundamental phenomenological level, the sense of ontological deficiency is experienced as: "There's something wrong with me." Thus, neo-Freudianism, like classical Augustinianism, impedes the development of the capacity for love.

There is another problem with the neo-Freudian anthropology-ontology. Even among the successfully psychoanalyzed elect, it cannot provide a foundation for a sense of self-worth. Its assumption of Darwinism makes it impossible for it to affirm the absolute worth of the individual, since human beings are putatively products of an accidental biological process bereft of intrinsic value. Only an ontology that is both theistic and humanistic can provide the foundation for self-respect, for dignity, and for a sense of spiritual well-being.

CHAPTER 8

Biological Psychiatry

Although biological psychiatry began to become a major force in the second half of the 20th century, and has stayed probably the dominant model, it is not a new development. Throughout the 20th century, mad people were assumed by hospital psychiatrists to be biologically abnormal, and were in fact effectively subdued by "somatic treatments." When psychiatry first emerged and began to claim the right to treat mad people, the model used was exclusively biological. Until Freud, virtually no one asserted that poor parenting was to blame for adults' problems.

The construction of private asylums for housing mad people began in Western Europe in the latter part of the 17th century and accelerated in the 18th century. Before that time, mad people were communal, monastic, and family responsibility and were kept in the community.[232] By the middle of the 18th century, legislation had been passed in England and France mandating the construction of county asylums to house pauper lunatics.

The latter part of the 19th century saw an increasingly concerted effort on the part of psychiatrists to define madness as a medical problem and to wrest control of public asylums from lay superintendents, who had control of virtually all of them; many of these superintendents were

232   Andrew Scull, *Social Order/Mental Disorder: Anglo-American Psychiatry in Historical Perspective* (Berkeley, California: University of California Press, 1989), p. 124.

committed to an approach to madness quite different from that of the psychiatrists: "moral management."

Moral management was the ideological rationale that was used in the first half of the 18th century to justify the construction of madhouses. Andrew Scull described it succinctly:

> It was a general pragmatic approach aimed at minimizing external, physical coercion; and it has therefore usually been interpreted as unproblematically kind and humane. Instead of merely resting content with controlling those who were no longer quite human, which had been the dominant concern of traditional responses to the mad, moral treatment actively sought to transform the lunatic, to remodel him or her into something approximating the bourgeois ideal of the rational individual; and as part of this process, an effort was made to create an environment that removed the artificial obstacles standing in the way of the "natural" tendencies toward recovery.[233]

Pioneers of this method were remarkably successful in eliminating the manifestations of social deviance and in motivating their patients to return to work.

Psychiatrists at first reluctantly accepted moral management, and acknowledged its utility when combined with medical treatments. By the mid-19th century, however, psychiatrists began to view the moral approach to insanity as an obstacle, both to enhancing their own professional status as experts on the treatment of the insane—doctors of the mad occupied the lowest and least prestigious rung on the professional ladder—and of wrenching control of asylums away from non-physicians.

233 Ibid., p. 129.

Doctors of the mad coordinated their efforts in a drive to establish their authority and to secure recognition of the disease model of madness. In 1844 the newly formed Association for Medical Superintendents of American Institutions for the Insane began publication of the *American Journal of Insanity*. The British counterpart of this association began publishing *Journal of Mental Science* in 1853. The editorial of the second volume declared, "Insanity is purely a disease of the brain. The physician is now the responsible guardian of the lunatic and must ever remain so."[234]

The psychiatrists could have bolstered their position if they had been able to demonstrate that insanity was in fact caused by bio-physical variables. The problem was that as hard as they tried, they were unable to show the existence of physical lesions in the brain. As one psychiatrist wrote in the late 19th century, "In three-fourths of the cases of insanity where they had been subjected to dissection after death, the knife of the anatomist has not been able, with the most scrutinizing care, to trace any organic change to which the cause of the disease could be traced."[235] The most common response to this failure was to argue that the existing instruments and techniques were too crude to detect the subtle changes in the brain that were the cause of insanity.

In their texts and publications, psychiatrists asserted with virtual unanimity that insanity was a somatic disease; the overwhelming majority believed that it was a disease of the brain, but a few doctors located the cause

234 Cited in Mary Boyle, *Schizophrenia; A Scientific Delusion?* (London: Routledge, 1990), p. 32.

235 Cited in Scull, *Social Order/Mental Disorder: Anglo-American Psychiatry in Historical Perspective*, p. 155.

elsewhere (either in the stomach or in the blood). In the meantime, in their publications and professional demeanor, psychiatrists endeavored to *appear* as much like ordinary physicians as possible. "During the second half of the 19th century, asylum doctors increasingly behaved as if the inmates were literally sick. Microscopes became a standard part of asylum equipment; post-mortems were regularly performed to find the hypothesized brain lesions which were the cause of the inmates' strange behavior; it became commonplace for asylums to have their own laboratories and to emphasize the importance of histopathological (the changes in tissue caused by diseases) investigations; drugs were increasingly used to sedate the inmates....In order to convince the public and government that insanity was a medical matter, mad-doctors had to behave in the same fashion as their more secure colleagues who enjoyed the luxury of never, at least in recent history, having had to convince people that bodily ailments were a medical matter."[236]

Psychiatrists asserted the superiority of somatic treatments of insanity over that of moral management. The standard treatments at the time were bleeding, purges, vomits, and digitalis. In other words, patients were subjected needlessly to "treatments" that caused excessive pain, anxiety, and/or discomfort and bodily harm. The prolific psychiatrist James Pritchard claimed in the mid-19th century to have witnessed a variety of cures from such treatments. His colleague Dr. John Thurnam was more circumspect. "Perhaps we can not produce any facts which actually prove that pharmaceutical treatment...has in any particular institution influenced the results on any large scale; yet

236 Boyle, *Schizophrenia: A Scientific Delusion?*, p. 34.

we can not doubt that the proportion of recoveries is greater...in a hospital for the insane, in which attention is paid to a discriminating and judicious medical treatment."[237]

Not only did somatic treatments make patients easier to warehouse and manage, but they bolstered mad-doctors own role identity as doctors in their own minds and in that of the public. It is for the same reasons that insulin shock and lobotomies were so widely utilized by psychiatrists in the mid-20th century. Psychiatrist Roy Grinker attributed the "rapidity" of the spread of insulin treatment throughout the United States to "the preparedness and eagerness of the rank and file psychiatrist for an organic approach to psychosis."[238] Professor of psychology Elliot Valenstein, in his authoritative history of psycho-surgery, attributed the popularity of electroshock and lobotomies among psychiatrists to the fact that "by using these somatic techniques, psychiatrists felt they were brought closer to the mainstream of medicine from which they often felt isolated."[239]

Despite the lofty claims of medical efficacy, the purpose of such treatments seemed to be to so pacify mad persons that they would remain docile and indifferent in an environment where the sanest among us would find it difficult "to resist the horrible influence of the place," as John Connolly, professor of medicine in London in the mid-19th century, put it. He stated, "Confinement is the very reverse of beneficial. It fixes and renders permanent what

237 Cited in Scull, *Social Order/Mental Disorder: Anglo-American Psychiatry in Historical Perspective*, p. 158.

238 Elliot Valenstein, *Great and Desperate Cures* (New York: Basic Books, 1986), p. 17.

239 Ibid., p. 177.

might have passed away."[240] Confinement in these institutions, he argued were "ruining" both the bodies and minds of the inmates.

By the end of the 19th century the asylum doctors "were now able to drive competing lay people out of the same line of work and to subordinate those who stayed in the field to their authority."[241] For a variety of reasons, the growth of the psychoanalytic movement did not undermine this authority but further reinforced it.

It should be emphasized that psychiatry's success in gaining control over the field of mental health in the 19th century, sustained throughout the 20th century, resulted not from any superior competence in understanding or resolving the problems of its patients/clients, but rather because of its superior moral entrepreneurship (to use Scull's term), an activity "in which power and persuasive rhetoric were of greater importance than the objective character of the knowledge, training, and work."[242]

The Resurgence of Biological Psychiatry

Despite their divergent theoretical explanations for mental distress, biological psychiatry coexisted peacefully with psychoanalysis throughout the 20th century. In the first place, psychoanalysts did not encroach upon the territory of biological psychiatry, as they regarded mental patients as irreversibly mentally ill, and thus not suitable candidates for psychoanalysis. Although many psychoanalytic

240 Cited in Scull, *Social Order/Mental Disorder: Anglo-American Psychiatry in Historical Perspective*, pp. 45-46.
241 Ibid., p. 161.
242 Ibid., p. 161.

mental health professionals worked in mental hospitals—
at least at the beginning of their careers before they built
up a private practice of more prestigious clients—they
rarely, if ever, challenged the use of the brain-damaging
procedures with which biological psychiatrists "treated"
their patients, such as electroshock and psycho-surgery.
Furthermore, although Freudians denied that "psychopathology" had an organic etiology, their use of medical terminology bolstered the status of psychiatrists. Against
Freud's own wishes, the most prestigious training insti-
tutes in psychoanalysis restricted (until recently) entrance
to physicians!

By the 1930s state mental hospitals in America and
Europe had become increasingly crowded and difficult to
manage. These institutions have been compared to con-
centration camps. Conditions were unsanitary, the diet was
so impoverished that many patients suffered from malnu-
trition, there were virtually no occupational or recreational
opportunities, a normal sexual life was impossible, and
the low-paid ward personnel had no qualms about using
violence to maintain "law and order."

The 1930s marked a change in the fashion of control-
ling mental patients—or in their "psychiatric treatment,"
to use the terminology of the "mental health" professionals. In previous years, treatment consisted of assaults on
the patients' bodies: Patients were shackled, whipped, immersed in ice cold water, bled, placed in straightjackets
and in solitary confinement.[243] As Breggin notes, "But
with the third decade of the 20th century, psychiatrists

243 See Peter Breggin, *Electro-Shock: Its Brain Disabling Effects*
(New York: Springer Publishing Co., 1990), pp. 136-138.

BIOLOGICAL PSYCHIATRY

discovered it was more efficient to attack the brain directly."[244] The first breakthrough had taken place in 1928, when a psychiatrist discovered that overdosing addicts with insulin made them more docile and manageable. The widespread acceptance of insulin shock therapy paved the way for the "treatment" most popular in the 1940s: the lobotomy.

During the 1940s and early 1950s, approximately fifty thousand lobotomies were performed on schizophrenics. In 1949, the inventor of the lobotomy, Egas Moniz, was awarded the Nobel Prize for his "miracle cure." By the mid-1950s, the lobotomy craze was over and there were probably few psychiatrists who would publicly defend the operation.

The neuroleptic ("anti-psychotic") drugs that were introduced into mental hospitals in the 1950s made ward management easier, but it did little for the patients. The psychiatrists who first introduced these drugs into the United States noted that their effects—loss of initiative, of abstract thinking, of motivation, and of creativity—were similar to that of the lobotomy.[245]

In the 1960s, for the first time, a threat to the power of psychiatry began to develop. In the early 1960s, Thomas Szasz and others presented new models for understanding the problems of life, models that refrained from interpreting deviant or troublesome behavior as symptoms of illnesses. About the same time, pioneers in the family therapy movement—Salvador Minuchin, Jay Haley, Virginia Satir—discovered that thinking of their patients'

244 Ibid., p. 137.
245 Peter Breggin, *Psychiatric Drugs: Hazards to the Brain* (New York: Springer Publishing Company, 1985), pp. 12-18.

emotional problems as diseases impeded their ability to help identify and solve them. They realized that a wide range of "acting out" or "crazy" behavior actually emerged from conflicts between family members . Their patients required conflict resolution, not medical diagnoses.

By the early 1970s, as Peter Breggin points out in *Toxic Psychiatry*, "The American Psychiatric Association was in financial trouble. It was losing membership and its total income was $2 – $4 million per year compared to its current income of over $21 million. In general, psychiatry was losing badly in the competition with psychologists, social workers, counselors, family therapists, and other non-medical professionals who charged lower fees."[246] At the same time, a small group within the profession was criticizing the American Psychiatric Association's relationship with the pharmaceutical industry. In response to these criticisms, the APA formed a "Task Force to Study the Impact of Potential Loss of Pharmaceutical Support." The task force concluded that many local APA member organizations and various training programs would fold without drug company support.

Breggin summarized the developments that took place:

> The floodgates of drug company influence were opened and...would grow wider each year. Nowadays, dozens of seminars are supported by the drug companies and the individual names of the companies are honored conspicuously with advertisements in psychiatric journals and newspapers prior to the meetings.... [247]

246   Peter Breggin, *Toxic Psychiatry* (New York: St. Martin's Press, 1991), p. 354.
247 Ibid.

In 1980 the APA voted to encourage pharmaceutical companies to support scientific or cultural activities rather than strictly social activities as a part of the annual meeting program....

> Whatever function APA had ever filled as a professional organization was now superseded by its function as a political advocate for the advancement of psychiatric and pharmaceutical business interests. Continually reiterated is the conviction that only a medical or biological image can enable psychiatry to compete economically.[248]

Behind the economic threat lay an even more ominous threat: a threat to the very identity of psychiatry as a field of medical specialization. This threat reached a pitch in the writing of Thomas Szasz and R.D. Laing, both of whom denied the existence of mental illness and even dared to claim that the psychiatrist's paradigmatic Other, the schizophrenic, was a fellow human being and the moral and ontological equal of the psychiatrist. But if the madman was only different, then psychiatry lost its hold upon the very symbolism that constituted its identity and vested it with spiritual significance as a source of social security: medical doctors battling valiantly against a mental illness so severe that it could vitiate a person's very humanity, and which could only be contained by Medical Science itself. To counter these threats, the psychiatric industry, financed by the pharmaceutical companies, launched what one psychiatrist aptly termed "the most successful marketing campaign, in terms of research dollars, political

248   Ibid., pp. 354-355.

power, and prestige, ever mounted by psychiatry."[249] According to Colin Ross, this marketing strategy includes the claims that "We are in the decade of the brain, that major discoveries are just around the corner, or that the latest brain scan or blood test is of fundamental interest."[250]

Madness as Mental Disease

The words of the 19th century psychiatric journal quoted earlier now appear prophetic: "Insanity is purely a disease of the brain. The physician is now the responsible guardian of the lunatic and must ever remain so." Psychologists, social workers, and other mental health professionals rarely bother to challenge this view, and have accepted their role as junior partners in the increasingly lucrative psychiatric-pharmaceutical complex.

Although a comprehensive critique of biological psychiatry is beyond the scope of this book, and has been mounted elsewhere,[251] hopefully a few comments will expose the dubious nature of biological psychiatry. In the first place, psychiatrists do not employ the same criteria that other physicians do in determining whether biological events are pathological. R.D. Laing clarified the difference, From a biological point of view, biological events are identified as pathological on biological grounds alone. Such are the only grounds for a biological judgment, but [in

249 Colin Ross and Alvin Pam, *Pseudo Science in Biological Psychiatry* (New York: John Wiley, 1995).

250 Ibid., p. 117.

251 See Peter Breggin, *Toxic Psychiatry* and Colin Ross and Alvin Pam, *Pseudoscience in Biological Psychiatry* (New York: John Wiley and Sons, 1995).

the case of psychiatry] it hardly seems that the biological judgment is based on biological criteria. It is because we regard some experiences as worthless, and destructive *per se*, that we feel that the biological processes that accompany them *must* be pathological. That is to say, whatever biological changes may be thought or found to engender, occasion, or accompany experience, the judgment that the biological sequence is dysfunctional, or pathological, is based on the view that the experience is dysfunctional, or psycho-pathological.[252]

E. Fuller Torrey succumbs to just such spurious reasoning in his attempt to prove that schizophrenia is a brain disease. The salient features of this disease, Torrey states, are enlarged ventricles.[253] But as John Modrow points out, a number of studies have shown that "normal" individuals frequently have enlarged ventricles. *Thus, enlarged ventricles cannot in and of themselves be taken as proof that there has been brain damage.* Furthermore, in the majority of magnetic resonance imaging brain scan studies, it has been found that a clear majority of the "schizophrenics" had normal-sized ventricles.[254]

An enormous amount of research has gone into establishing a hereditability factor for schizophrenia. As noted above, this does not bear on whether the issue of schizophrenia is a disease, although psychiatric propaganda implies that it does. It is notable that though these studies have been shown to be seriously flawed method-

252 R.D. Laing, *The Voice of Experience* (New York: St. Martin's Press, 1991), p. 43.

253 See John Modrow, *How to Become a Schizophrenic* (Everett, Washington: Apollyon Press, 1992), pp. 166-168.

254 Ibid., p. 166.

ologically by numerous authors including Ross and Pam,[255] they are cited in psychiatric textbooks as revealed truth.

Psychiatry's strongest argument that schizophrenia is a disease is the claim that they discovered a cure for it in the early 1950s. In actuality, the word *cure* is used only occasionally—more often they state that "anti-psychotic medication" keeps the disease under control—they almost invariably add, just as insulin controls diabetes. This is an unassailable article of faith in the mental health profession, with only a handful of dissenters challenging this dogma.[256]

Psychiatry's coalition with the pharmaceutical companies have provided it with the financial resources it needed to launch a major public relations campaign to convince the public that "schizophrenics" and sufferers from other "mental illness" are biologically inferior: Their abhorrent behavior is the result of defective genes. Psychiatrists usually hasten to add that this is a more "humane" explanation than the older Freudian theory, since it does not "blame the parents." After all, it is not the parents' fault that they passed on "bad" genes. With this new approach the American Psychiatric Association has been able to sell schizophrenia to the parents and relatives of individuals undergoing spiritual crises. They have successfully organized an organization (National Alliance of the Mentally Ill) comprised of over a hundred thousand parents and other family members of "the mentally ill" who engage in

255   Ross and Pam, *Pseudoscience in Biological Psychiatry*, pp. 10-37.

256   Peter Breggin, *Psychiatric Drugs: Hazards to the Brain*, and Seth Farber, *Madness, Heresy and the Rumor of Angels: The Revolt Against the Mental Health System* (Chicago: Open Court, 1993).

various activities designed to garner support for the agenda of psychiatry. (The parents of one of my clients, John, a diagnosed "schizophrenic"—when I worked in New Jersey—enthusiastically attended their support group meetings regularly. John rebelled and thwarted their plans to launch him on a career as a chronic mental patient. He discontinued the drugs, took up a trade, and today owns his own carpentry company.)

Claims of inferiority are very persuasive when they are couched in medical terminology, as medicine is considered a "hard" science. Thus despite the failure to prove that "schizophrenia" is caused by a biological defect, and despite the massive data contradicting this interpretation (e.g., individuals who reject the mental health system tend to "get better"), most Americans have been convinced that it has been proven that schizophrenia is a medical disease.

Like the neo-Freudians, the biological psychiatrists ignore factors in individuals' present environment that could explain their distress or unhappiness. As noted above, in Freud's analysis of Dora, the grand master seemed to suffer from a congenital blindness to the kinds of "environmental factors" (e.g., deceit, misogyny, sexual exploitation) that one would expect to cause distress in "normal" subjects. If Dora had had the opportunity to consult one of today's biological psychiatrists, she might have been diagnosed as suffering from a "mood disorder" and placed on Prozac.

I want to emphasize that the attribution of pathology almost always rests on the positivist premise that an individual's difficulty adjusting to his environment is *ipso facto* evidence of a biologically based mental disorder. The diagnosis is never determined by examination of biological variables; it is always inferred from the presence of unwanted behavior. The conformist nature of the mental health system was tersely and unwittingly revealed by the comments in 1974 of the British psychiatrist William Sargent, who in praising the advances of modern psychiatry wrote that "Jesus Christ might simply have returned to His carpentry following the use of modern psychiatric treatments."[257] Undoubtedly, most mental health professionals would have regarded this as a great accomplishment—to be able to have transformed the Messiah into an ordinary carpenter, thus preventing the Crucifixion (and the Resurrection). Dr. Sargent neglected to mention that Jesus would have needed to continue to take His "meds," lest he have a relapse and become a troublemaker again. In more general terms, we could say that this is in fact the agenda of psychiatry: to reduce the extraordinary to the ordinary, the poetic to the banal, to transform prophets, mystics, and revolutionaries into drudges and conformists.

The Premises of Biological Psychiatry

The Augustinian-Freudian idea that the soul or psyche is damaged, that the individual's worth is diminished is modified by biological psychiatry since it relies upon a jargon that is lacking in spiritual or religious resonance. The root metaphor in this theory is functionality: Some human beings are functional, but most are dysfunctional to a greater or lesser degree.

Second, Nature makes mistakes (it is sometimes implied that this is an inevitable result of the evolutionary

257 William Sargent, "The Movement in Psychiatry," *The Times* (English), August 22, 1974, p. 14.

process): These mistakes are termed "genetic flaws," and they lead individuals to develop "bio-chemical imbalances" that prevent them from being fully adaptive.

Third, there is a complex stratification of individuals, but there is only one fundamental distinction between two groups: the seriously mentally ill, and those with more minor bio-chemical imbalances that prevent optimal functioning. The imbalances of the latter group can be entirely corrected with the proper psychiatric medication. The former group consists of the "chronically mentally ill," and medication can only ameliorate their suffering: They remain unfit.

This paradigm does not imply the transcendence of nature in any way comparable to modern Freudianism. Unlike neo-Freudianism which holds human beings (parents) responsible for "pathology," biological psychiatry regards nature as so fundamentally flawed that it produces copious "genetic defects" among the human population. On the other hand, despite the imperfection of nature, biological psychiatry maintains that the psychiatrist working with nature can help individuals to overcome their "biochemical imbalances," thus restoring the balance that nature manifests in its more successful human products.

There is not the same preoccupation with sin and defect that one finds in Freudianism, because biological psychiatry is almost entirely bereft of all concepts that have any kind of conscious or unconscious religious implications. It does not appeal to the human yearning for individual salvation as Freudianism does. It merely promises to enable many individuals to function as more efficient machines, with a greater degree of comfort.

PART THREE

CHAPTER 9

The Church Versus
the Service Professions

The most typical objection to those who argue that Christians ought to assume responsibility for ministering to the emotional and spiritual needs of each other is that the Christian priest, monk, nun, or layperson does not possess the competence of the highly educated, highly trained, experienced mental health scientist-professional.

In 1977, Mary L. Smith and Gene V. Glass published an article in *American Psychologist* that summarized the results of 375 studies of psychotherapy. Although they concluded that therapy was effective, they also discovered that the therapist's credentials—Ph.D., M.D., or no advanced degree—and experience were *unrelated* to the efficacy of therapy. Psychologist Robyn Dawes re-evaluated these studies and other studies in 1979 and came to the same conclusion: "Although therapy is effective in eliminating symptoms, the credentials and experience of the therapist don't matter."[258]

Since this result is unpleasant for professionals who require years of post-graduate training and post-doctoral experience for licensing, and who would like to restrict the practice of therapy to those who are licensed, many attempts have been made since the Smith and Glass article was first published to disprove their findings. As

258   Robyn Dawes, *House of Cards* (New York: Free Press, 1994), p. 54.

Dawes demonstrates, these attempts failed. Psychologist Jerome Frank also acknowledged "the inability of scientific research to demonstrate conclusively that professional psychotherapists produce results sufficiently better than those of non-professionals."[259]

Another significant finding is that all forms of therapy are equally effective. Morris Parloff, former chief of the Psycho-Social Treatment Research branch of the National Institute of Mental Health stated, "Nearly five hundred rigorously controlled studies have shown with almost monotonous regularity that all forms of psychological treatment...are comparably effective."[260]

The obvious interpretation of this finding is that nonspecific factors independent of any particular form of therapy—or of "non-professional" human relationships—account for the beneficial changes. Research studies (that will not be presented here)—and common sense—indicates that the two most salient nonspecific factors are the interpersonal qualities of the counselor, and the arousal of positive expectations, as in the placebo effect. Research has consistently shown that therapists who are perceived as warm, empathic, and genuine are more likely to produce positive changes in their clients. As Martin and Deirdre Bobgan note, "All of these factors are at play in all effective human relationships. None of these factors require psychological training, psychological techniques, psychological degrees, or psychological licensing."[261]

It should be noted that the studies reviewed above

259 Martin and Deidre Bobgan, *Psychoheresy* (Santa Monica, California: EastGate Publishers, 1987), p. 180.
260 Cited in Bobgan, *Psychotherapy*, p. 183.
261 Ibid., p. 187.

made no attempt to assess the potentially adverse effects of therapy on the percentage of clients who did not improve. Furthermore, the conditions of these studies minimize the possibility of adverse effects, as the vast majority of outcome studies were done in academic settings, where treatment is closely monitored, guided by well-designed procedures, and reviewed by supervisors. They are thus subject to "quality control" that is not available to the large majority of individuals who are treated in clinics. Second, these studies specifically excluded the kinds of clients that therapists have the most destructive impact upon: those deemed "mentally ill." Third, the studies were done within narrow parameters: They obviously did not attempt to assess the overall impact of psychotherapy upon a society in which it has been embraced as a panacea for all social ills.

Nonetheless, the implications of these studies are profound: They call into question the very nature of the therapeutic enterprise, and undermine the credibility of the mental health system's program for the betterment of society. The research demonstrates unequivocally that psychology while promoting idolatry of Science—of which it claims to be an exemplar—has itself no scientific foundation. A highly educated and "scientifically trained" and licensed psychotherapist is no more likely than an amateur with no training whatsoever to be an effective agent of change.

The Psychological Seduction of Christianity

It is not surprising that the mental health industry has made no policy changes as a result of these findings. It is however disappointing, if not surprising, that those calling themselves Christians have not been emboldened by these conclusions to assert their distinctive identity as agents for social and spiritual transformation. Rather than daring to follow in the path of Her Lord, summoning individuals into Her salvific community, even the Orthodox Church seeks to enhance Her worldly glamour and acceptance by pursuing an alliance with Big Brother, the mental health system. Not a few priests pursue psychological studies, thinking this will enhance their ability to minister to the faithful. Has the Church forgotten yet once again, as She has often enough throughout history, that our Lord Himself was despised and crucified?

If not, then why has She ignored the warnings of prophets such as Martin and Deidre Bobgan? In their book *Psychoheresy, the Psychological Seduction of Christianity*, they document the tendency of Christians to be intimidated from "counseling"—helping—individuals due to their lack of "psychological training." Based on years of experience in the Christian Evangelical community, they conclude, "The most respected advice among Christians for problems of living is to 'get some counseling,' and by this they mean professional psychological counseling."[262] Priests and pastors are told repeatedly by psychologists, including psychologically trained priests or pastors, to refer individuals in distress to trained professionals. As one professor of psychology at a Protestant Christian college put it in 1983, "The pastor should be taught how to assemble a list of professionals in his community who will serve his parishioners well."[263] The Bobgans give several examples of this attitude among pastors—they state that they could

262 Ibid., p. 102.
263 Ibid., p. 104.

multiply examples of "the referral principle" but decided not to bore the reader since: "Everyone knows that the Church has become one gigantic referral service."[264] Sadly, what is true for many Protestants or Roman Catholics is also true to all too many Orthodox.

As the Bobgans document, not only does the Church refer troubled individuals to mental health professionals, but smitten by the power She seeks to emulate them, woo them, and is ready to sacrifice Her own identity in holy matrimony. An article in the *Christian Research Journal* corroborates this point: "Churches, Bible colleges and seminaries, Christian speakers, and Christian publishers across the country are promoting mental health programs to help Christians solve their personal problems and find personal fulfillment. Many Christian educational institutions have added psychology classes and majors, and some even have Masters and Ph.D. programs in psychology. Twelve Step programs patterned after Alcoholics Anonymous (AA) have been adapted by churches to address almost any kind of persistent personal problem, from obesity to 'spiritual' addictions. Some churches offer a personality evaluation with membership forms to ensure that new members have their emotional and mental health needs met in addition to their spiritual needs. There are even study Bibles designed especially for people 'in recovery.' Indeed, some Christians argue that inclusion of psychological principles and teachings into a biblical counseling setting is the only way to provide competent mental health care to Christians."[265]

264   Ibid., p. 110.
265   Bob and Gretchen Pasantino, "Psychology and the Church," *Christian Research Journal*, Winter 1995, p. 21.

Unfortunately, there are few voices like the Bobgans in the wilderness of Christianity today. Despite the growing destructiveness of the mental health system, and the undeniable evidence that the credentials of mental health professionals are not reflective of specialized competence, Christians continue to turn to Freudians, Jungians, and Rogerian-trained therapists.

The Defense of Community and the Critique of Professionalism

Professionalism has undermined the Church's autonomy of dominant social institutions and compromised Her ability to act as a prophetic critic of the social order. Thus, with the exception of the Bobgans, the most perceptive critics of the deleterious impact of the mental health professions on the vitality of community and the task of creating a participatory democracy have not identified themselves as Christians. One such critic is William Schambra, a conservative inspired by the work of Robert Nesbitt, who calls for a "new citizenship" whose goal is "the reconstruction of civil society, the return of America to the self-governing republic described by Alexis de Tocqueville and envisioned by the Founding Fathers."[266] Schambra believes that this new citizenship will need to roll back "the incursions of the therapeutic state into the everyday lives of Americans by challenging the political hegemony of the 'helping' and 'caring' professions and bureaucracies. This requires dramatizing their status as entrenched corrupt special interests more concerned about

266 William Shambra, "By The People," in *Policy Review*, Summer 1994, p. 32.

advancing narrow ideological agendas and protecting political prerogatives than about the public."[267]

At the other end of the political spectrum, the late Christopher Lasch reached a similar conclusion. In Lasch's book *The Revolt of the Elites and the Betrayal of Democracy*, he described critically the transformation of the United States from a self-governing republic where "even the humbler members of society" had "access to the knowledge and cultivation" required for active citizenship to a "therapeutic state" ruled by managerial elites increasingly insulated by their culture and lifestyle from the concerns of the rest of the people.[268] Denouncing "the reign of specialized expertise,"[269] he asked, "Is it really necessary to point out at this late date that public policies based on a therapeutic model have failed miserably over and over again? Far from promoting self-respect, they have created a nation of dependents....The professionalization of compassion...institutionalizes inequality."[270]

Paul Piccone and his colleagues at *Telos* journal have developed a sophisticated critique of the welfare state and pseudo-democratic modes of "New Class" domination. Federal intervention have less to do with securing equal rights for everyone "than with the implementation of a New Class agenda of securing the privileges of middle-class intellectuals running state agencies and bureaucracies at the expense of an increasingly clientized popu-

267 Ibid., p. 32.
268 Christopher Lasch, *The Revolt of the Elites and the Betrayal of Democracy* (New York: W.W. Norton and Company, 1995), p. 58.
269 Ibid., p. 79.
270 Ibid., p. 211.

lace."[271] *Telos* was founded in the late 1960s by Piccone as a "new left" journal; Piccone now maintains that the distinction between "left" and "right" is meaningless, and advocates for a renewed "populism" uniting all individuals favoring "local autonomy, fiscal austerity and participatory forms of democrary."[272]

James Hillman, a Jungian psychologist for several decades, stopped practicing therapy about seven years ago. He became so disturbed by the effects of what he terms the "therapeutic ideology," which leads people to believe that the source of all their problems lies within them, as a result of events that happened in the past. He maintains that this obscures the political nature of human existence. He argues that the "recovery movement" has become a national obsession, as millions of people get together to commiserate with each other about their common victimhood: as children of alcoholics, as food addicts, as recovering alcoholics, as people who need other people, i.e., co-dependents. Hillman says, "For everyone to sit around a room because they're fat—I don't know if that's a way a civilization can continue." He suggests as an alternative, "Suppose we begin seeing ourselves not as patients, but as citizens."[273]

Wendy Kaminer is similarly critical of the recovery movement in her book *I'm Dysfunctional, You're Dysfunctional*. She states, "With the rise of a personal development

271 Paul Piccone, "Rethinking Federalism," *Telos*, Vol. 100, Summer 1994, p. 6.
272 Paul Piccone, "Confronting the French New Right," *Telos*, 98-9, Winter 1993-Spring 1994.
273 James Hillman, "The Rainmaker Phantasy," in *The Family Therapy Networker*, Volume 15, No. 5. Sept./Oct. 1991, p. 64.

movement centered around victimization, victimology can fairly be called a study of our culture."[274] She questions, "What are the political implications of a mass movement that counsels surrender of will and submission to a higher power describing almost everyone as hapless victims of familial abuse?...The notion of selfhood that emerges from recovery (the most vulgarized renditions of salvation by grace, positive thinking, and mind cure) is essentially more conducive to totalitarianism than democracy."[275] (It should be noted, in fairness, that the actual practices of most twelve step groups are often democratic in nature—in spite of their victimological anthropology.)

Mental health professionals and other self-help gurus prey upon what I have termed feelings of deficiency that I believe are vestiges of our culture molded for centuries by an Augustinian anthropology. One psychologist who had been in therapy for twenty years herself wrote, "While I was in therapy I enjoyed the attention my therapist provided me....I became addicted to this attention, and to keep it, I remain in the role of the dependent one, needing validation and almost by definition feeling insufficient. I pathologized myself to remain in treatment."[276]

John McKnight argues that the welfare state and the ideology of professionalism are the primary obstacle to the reconstitution of communities and the reconstruction of democracy in the United States. He writes, "The enemy is

274   Wendy Kaminer, *I'm Dysfunctional; You're Dysfunctional* (New York: Addison-Wesley, 1992), p. 154.

275   Ibid., p. 152.

276   Cited in Tana Dineen, *Manufacturing Victims: What the Psychology Industry is Doing to People* (Toronto: Robert Davies, 1996), p. 238.

not poverty, sickness and disease. The enemy is a set of interests that need dependency masked by service."[277] Along with Lasch, McKnight regards the definition of social problems in medical terms as the prerequisites for stripping individuals of their citizenship and permanently relegating them to an inferior caste of "clients." Whatever resources or "services" they are then "entitled to" cannot compensate for this degradation. He succinctly describes the therapeutic ideology as follows: "(1) The basic problem is you, (2) the resolution of your problem is my professional control, and (3) my control is your help...."[278]

McKnight rejects "the therapeutic vision," which sees "the well-being of individuals as growing from an environment composed of professionals and their services. It envisions a world where there is a professional to meet every need and where the fee to secure each professional service is a right."[279]

The only genuine solution, McKnight argues, is the realization of the "community vision," which requires, as he says, "the conversion of clients to citizens."[280] The community vision seeks to relocate power from the centralized and professionally dominated service system to "neighborhood associations," which by his definition range from churches to the neighborhood taverns, where two centuries ago "some of the most basic discussions about the formation of the government of the United States and its Constitution occurred."[281]

277 John McKnight, *The Careless Society; Community and its Counterfeits* (New York: Basic Books, 1995), p. 98.
278 Ibid., p. 61.
279 Ibid., 168.
280 Ibid., p. 62.
281 Ibid., p. 118.

The community vision seeks to provide every citizen, no matter how "fallible," the opportunity to participate as a political equal with other citizens in the process of community decision-making and neighborhood-building. It seeks to "recommunalize" exiled and psychiatrically-labelled individuals. "It sees the community associations as contexts in which to create and locate jobs, provide opportunities for recreation of multiple friendships, and become the political defender of the right of labelled people to be free from exile [from the community]."[282]

It is ironic and tragic that at a time when advanced social thinkers such as Lasch and McKnight have critiqued the pretensions of psychology and exposed the dangerously anti-democratic nature of the helping professions at a time when the research published by mental health professionals themselves cannot validate the efficacy of their higher training, even within their own narrow terms, that Christians opt for professionalism over democracy and are seduced by the prospect of building yet another growth industry: Christian psychology. Even the Orthodox Church frequently underestimated the resources of Her own salvific community and vacillates between the ideals of Christ and the Fathers and the ideals of Freud or Jung, and is seduced by the prospect of becoming yet another growth industry.

Restoring the Authority of the Christian Community

The Church's first task is to be the Church, to be that community faithful to the way of Jesus, to the Kingdom of God, to be a new polis (to use one of Hauerwas' favorite

282 Ibid., p. 169.

phrases).[283] The creation of a viable Christian community is not a substitute for missionary activity, but the precondition for it. As Charles Scriven puts it, the Body of Christ must be both an "alternative society" and a "transformative example"—"the light of the world," "a city on the hill."[284] The Christian community then must become the vanguard of the new order that establishes "beachheads" (to use Beker's term) of the Kingdom of God in the enemy camp, in "this world."[285]

Theologian Thomas Finger explains in a very concrete manner the way in which Christians can transform the world. Christians must provide visions of alternative ways in which life can be lived, and they must then make them "actual possibilities in which people are invited to participate."[286] The Christian community can have the most powerful transformative impact upon the world not by helping its "present structures to function better" but by presenting it with new alternative possibilities that conform to the Christian ideal of the Kingdom of God on earth. These alternative models can break through the world's "systemic blindness and initiate social changes which might never have occurred otherwise."[287]

This model requires that the Church create alternatives to the mental health system, e.g., alternatives to

283 Stanley Hauerwas and William H. Willimon, *Resident Aliens* (Nashville, Tennessee: Abingdon Press, 1989).

284 Charles Scriven, *The Transformation of Culture* (Scottdale, Pennsylvania: Herald Press, 1988), p. 181.

285 Beker, *Paul the Apostle: The Triumph of God in Life and Thought* (Philadelphia, Pennsylvania: Fortress Press, 1980), pp. 318-319.

286 Thomas Finger, *Christian Theology: An Eschatological Approach, Volume 2*, p. 287.

287 Ibid., p. 289.

mental hospitals and psychiatric wards. The goal of these alternative structures should be twofold: (1) to help individuals resolve their crises; and (2) to facilitate individuals' eventual incorporation into the Church, as a counterculture to the world. (Some individuals will choose not to become Christians. They should not be coerced, but they should be offered this option.) The countercultural model is not compatible with the Church's present policy of deferring the responsibility of caring for individuals who are experiencing distress or crises to the secular mental health experts.

This policy conflicts with the Christian mission, which is first of all eschatological: to prepare individuals to live in accord with new norms, and to integrate them into a community oriented toward the Kingdom of God. My argument is that Christians in general, and Orthodox in particular, cannot reconcile this goal with the current practice of referring individuals who are experiencing emotional distress to mental health professionals. The premise that I assume underlies this practice strikes me as completely schizophrenic: mental health professionals are the most qualified to take care of individuals' emotional or "clinical" needs, whereas the Church can take care of their "spiritual" needs.[288]

While the individual is seeing a mental health professional to resolve his emotional problems, a minister

288 It is important to note that the word *clinical* in this context has no substantive meaning. Mental health professionals use it to assert in disguise what they regard as their prerogatives. Thus, if an individual is suffering from a "clinical depression," he clearly needs to be seen by a professional. While this usage implies that there are ordinary "non-clinical" depressions, I have never heard a mental health professional speak of one.

or pastor or priest typically will tell him that he is welcome to attend church services in order to meet his spiritual needs. If the individual is in severe distress, he will have to wait until he is released from the psychiatric ward of the hospital to have his spiritual needs satisfied by attending church services—unless, of course, the psychiatric authorities believe that he is "healthy" enough to offer him a pass to attend church.

Christians have no justification for referring emotionally distressed individuals to therapists or to psychiatric wards.[289] They do not have the kind of expertise that they are universally assumed to possess. More importantly, as I noted above, the therapist's allegiance is to his profession, not to building up the Church as a counterculture loyal to the way of Christ.

There is a stark contrast between the practice of Jesus

289 I will argue in more detail later that the Church should establish alternative asylums for individuals who are undergoing emotional or spiritual crises. I think that they should also have access when experiencing severe distress to the least toxic tranquilizers (not the neuroleptic drugs that are usually forced upon "patients"). Thus there will need to be a medical doctor on hand who has the power to prescribe tranquilizing drugs to patients. Also, I believe that family therapists may be able to help identify and resolve or negotiate conflicts within a family. I want to add that graduate degrees are not necessary for training as a family therapist, although most training programs require them. The renowned family therapist Jay Haley once said (personal communication) that professionals with graduate school education were the most difficult to train as family therapists because they had been most indoctrinated in the mental illness model. For the difference between a real family therapist—who actually empowers the family—and those who actually adhere to a more traditional model, I refer the reader to the book by psychologist Terence Cambell, Ph.D., *Beware of the Talking Cure* (Boca Raton, Florida: Social Issue Resource Series, 1994).

and the practice of all Christian bodies today, including Orthodoxy. People who sought to be accepted in Christ's community included tax collectors, prostitutes, "sinners" of all varieties, outcasts, misfits, individuals who were regarded as "impure" in a manner analogous to the way mental patients are today. Like mental patients, they were exiles, not merely in the sense that Israel was in exile, but from their own community. Jesus invited them to His table, into His community, to His party celebrating the Kingdom of God. He did not say to them, "First go back to the Pharisees to be purified and then come back to me and I will take care of your spiritual needs." (Nor did Paul say that.) The means of purification were open to them in principle within the existing sacrificial system.[290] Jesus offered the blessings of the Kingdom of God "outside the official structures, to all the wrong people, on His own authority."[291] It is a tragic comment on the influence of secularism among all Christian bodies, including Orthodoxy, that they are ready to so severely undermine their own authority by giving their endorsement to the "official structures," which exist for the purpose of stabilizing a corrupt social order. Christians cannot build a strong distinctive counterculture in this fashion.

Former "mental patients" are defined and treated by the mental health professions (and society) as defective. They are thus denied the opportunity to engage in socially valued work, or to be a contributing member to a non-stigmatized community. This is what they yearn for and need the most, the opportunity to be "recommunalized"

290 N.T. Wright, *Jesus and the Victory of God* (Minneapolis, Minnesota: Fortress Press, 1996), p. 274.
291 Ibid., p. 272.

CHAPTER NINE

(to borrow a term from social critic John McKnight). Those who advocate such a policy "see a society where those who were once labeled, exiled, treated, counseled, advised, and protected are, instead, incorporated into community, where their contributions, capacities, gifts, and fallibilities will allow a network of relationships involving work, recreation, friendship, support, and the political power of being a citizen."[292] It is our responsibility as Christians to give this opportunity to society's pariahs.

St. Paul understood well that persons attained maturity using the gifts that had been given to them by Christ. These gifts were that "some should be apostles, some prophets, some evangelists, some priests and teachers...for building up the Body of Christ...until we all attain to the unity of the faith and the knowledge of the Son of God...to the measure of the stature of the fullness of Christ" (Ephesians: 4: 11–13).

In R.D. Laing's book *The Politics of Experience,* he uses an illuminating metaphor.[293] He states that from an ideal vantage point on the ground, a formation of planes may be observed in the air. One plane may be out of formation, but the whole formation may be off course. The plane that is out of formation may be abnormal, bad, or mad from

292 John McKnight, *The Careless Society: Community and its Counterfeits* (New York: Basic Books, 1995), p. 169. See also Wolf Wolfensberger's important work *The New Genocide of Handicapped and Afflicted People* (Syracuse University, New York: Author, 1992). "Because genocide is so much an expression of imperial oppression and bureaucratized stratification, it is also important to respond by creating and practicing communality, both with other like-minded people and with people at risk" (p. 87).

293 R.D. Laing, *The Politics of Experience* (New York: Pantheon Books, 1967), p. 120.

the point of view of the formation, but the formation may be bad or mad from the point of view of the ideal observer. The plane that is out of formation may be more on course than the formation itself is.

Laing states that the "out of formation" criterion is a clinical positivist criterion, whereas the "off course" criterion is the ontological. From our perspective, we can say that the "off course" criterion is the Christian.

From the Christian perspective, we know the formation, "this world," is off course. The Church Herself is—at Her best—out of formation but on course. The professional psychologist may or may not help the client get back into formation, but he is neither inclined nor likely to help the person get back on course. It is the role of the Church to help individuals get into Her own formation—Her own countercultural community—and thus both in formation and on course.

CHAPTER 10

The Mental Patient as Exile, or as a Christian Initiate

The labelling of persons—as mentally healthy or diseased—constitutes the initial act of social validation and invalidation, pronounced by the high priest of modern, scientific religion, the psychiatrist; it justifies the expulsion of the sacrificial scapegoat, the mental patient, from the community.[294]

"Schizophrenia is the sacred symbol of psychiatry," Thomas Szasz wrote in 1976. [295] He wrote, "Schizophrenia has become the Christ on the cross that psychiatrists worship, in whose name they march in the battle to reconquer reason from unreason, sanity from insanity...reverence toward it has become the mark of psychiatric orthodoxy, and irreverence towards it the mark of psychiatric heresy."[296]

There are, of course, a plethora of studies claiming to have proven that "schizophrenia" is a disorder. Careful examination reveals that the data does not warrant this

294 Thomas Szasz, *The Manufacture of Madness: A Comparitive Study of the Inquisition in the Mental Health Movement* (New York: Harper and Row, 1970), p. 267.
295 See Thomas Szasz, *Schizophrenia: The Sacred Symbol of Pscyhiatry* (New York: Syracuse University Press, 1976).
296 Ibid., xvi.

conclusion.[297] Yet as a result of an advertising campaign by the American Psychiatric Association and their allies, aided by the assistance of the public media, virtually everyone assumes that it is a proven fact that thanks to scientific advances we now know that schizophrenia is a brain disorder. The views of dissenters in the field, such as Thomas Szasz or psychiatrist Peter Breggin, who attempted to expose the alliance of psychiatry with the pharmaceutical industry are not reviewed in any of the major presses.

David Cohen wrote, "The claim of mental illness-brain disease has been elevated to the status of nearly unchallengeable dogma that makes rejecting the somatic basis of schizophrenia equivalent to rejecting the somatic basis of diabetes."[298] This dogma includes the implication that this claim has not been made before. But, as indicated above, the very same dogma was promulgated in the 19th century and lingered on until Freudianism conquered the mental health field for a few decades with its own contention that "psychopathology" was caused by environmental factors.

Recently, psychiatry has incurred considerable criticism in the press since it decided to expand its empire and define everything from bad writing to shyness to playing video games as a mental disorder.[299] In the same year, 1994,

297 See, for example, Theodore R. Sarbin, "Toward the Obsolescence of the Schizophrenia Hypothesis," and Peter Breggin, "Brain Damage, Dementia and Persistent Cognitive Dysfunction Associated with Neuroleptic Drugs," David Cohen, ed., *Challenging the Therapeutic State, The Journal of Mind and Behavior,* Special Issue, Volume 11, Nos. 3-4, Summer-Autumn 1990, pp. 259-285 and pp. 425-465.
298 David Cohen, "Biological Basis of Schizophrenia: The Evidence Reconsidered," in *Social Work,* May 1989, p. 256.
299 American Psychiatric Association, *Diagnostic and Statistical*

a group of prominent mental health professionals published the results of their study in the prestigious *Archives of General Psychiatry*: Forty-eight percent of the population ostensibly suffers from a "lifetime psychiatric disorder."[300]

Beleaguered by skeptics, psychiatry is not about to abandon its strongest and most closely guarded fortress: Mental illness is a serious organic disorder requiring psychiatric treatment. After all, virtually no one, except a handful of heretics, questions this dogma, this article of faith, disguised as scientific fact. If psychiatry were forced to surrender on that battlefield and acknowledge that "chronic schizophrenia" is a social construction, their credibility would be completely undermined. The existence of their multi-million dollar empire (including the considerable financial interests of the pharmaceutical companies, hospitals, and non-medical professions) would be grossly threatened.

Furthermore, the very *identity* of the psychiatrist qua psychiatrist requires the existence of the schizophrenic. The psychiatrist sees himself, and is seen, as the agent of order and reason who protects society by using all his scientific powers to manage and constrain the pernicious and potentially explosive forces of chaos and irrationality represented by the schizophrenic, the lunatic.

My book *Madness, Heresy and the Rumor of Angels: A*

Manual of Mental Disorders, Fourth Edition (Washington, D.C.: American Psychiatric Association, 1994). See also article by L. J. Davis, "The Encyclopedia of Insanity," *Harper's Magazine*, February 1997, p. 61.

300 R. Kessler, et al, "Lifetime and Month Prevalence of the DSM3R Disorders in the United States: Results from the National Co-Morbidity Survey," in the *Archives of General Psychiatry*, Volume 1, January 1994, pp. 8-19.

Revolt Against the Mental Health System was a vigorous attack on the central dogma of psychiatry. My work as a therapist and my research had convinced me that "schizophrenia" is not a "chronic disease" but is rather an emotional and spiritual crisis precipitated by a traumatizing event or events in the individual's environment. The chronicity I demonstrated is created by the procedures of the mental health system itself.[301]

My book told the true stories of seven individuals, all of whom had psychotic breakdowns, and who met the psychiatric criteria for schizophrenia or other forms of "severe mental illness." Yet all of them "recovered"—that is, they resolved their crises. What did they do different from their more unfortunate peers? They extricated themselves from the mental health system and weaned

301 For additional confirmation that mental health professionals create the very "diseases" they claim to discover, the reader should consult Joan Acocella, "The Politics of Hysteria," in *The New Yorker*, April 6, 1998. The article demonstrates that the diagnosis of "multiple personality disorder" (MPD) is based on a false memory of sexual abuse planted (wittingly or unwittingly) in credulous women's minds by entrepreneurial therapists. Before 1975, cases of multiple personality disorder were so rare that the American Psychiatric Association did not even recognize its existence (p. 66). Shortly after it was recognized, it became an epidemic. Acocella reveals the dynamics of the creation of this disorder: credulous unhappy women went to therapists who specialized in the treatment of MPD, gave them books to read on the symptoms and prevalence of this disease, and succeeded easily in a context shaped by media hysteria (Oprah, Donahue, and Larry King all had shows on multiple personality disorders), both persuading them that they suffered from this affliction and inducing them to conform to the role expectations of the MPD personality. The influence of the media is demonstrated by the fact that between 1970 and 1990 the average annual output of publications on MPD increased six thousand percent (p. 66).

themselves off psychiatric drugs. (This should almost always be done slowly, and with social support, because these drugs are highly addictive and produce strong withdrawal effects.) Today they are living as "normal" people: They go to work or school, they have friends, are married or have intimate relationships. Since that time I have spoken to several hundred other individuals who have told me virtually the same story: They defied the commands of the psychiatric system, stepped out of the role of mental patient, and became indistinguishable from the "normal" population.

My argument that the chronicity of former "mental patients'" problems is created by the practices of psychiatry is supported by the voluminous literature on "experimenter bias." As Jerome Frank put it, "An experimenter's expectations can strongly bias the performance of his subjects by means of cues so subtle that neither experimenter nor subject need be aware of them."[302] Mental patients are not merely given subtle cues: Virtually all of them are told by every mental health professional they consult that they have a chronic mental illness. Clearly mental health professionals have low expectations for psychiatrically labelled individuals, expectations which powerfully influence their clients' ability to "perform" in life.

Jerome Frank, in his review of the literature on therapist/patient relations, wrote, "A therapist cannot avoid biasing his patient's performance in accordance with his own expectations...."[303] He added that his influence is heightened not only by his role and his status but by his attitude

302 Jerome Frank, *Persuasion in Healing* (New York: Schocken Books, 1974), p. 127.
303 Jerome Frank, *Persuasion in Healing*, pp. 127-128.

of concern and his patient's vulnerability. The implication of this is that the more strongly bonded a former mental patient is with his therapist—who almost always has low expectations of mental patients—the more likely he is to act as mental patients are expected to act.

Psychiatric Myths

The "mentally ill" are among us now; they no longer languish in back wards of state mental hospitals. Their evident misery is impossible to ignore. But according to the propagandists of the mental health system, assisted by their acolytes in the media, in the late 1950s and early 1960s mental health professionals began a process of "deinstitutionalization" designed to integrate mental patients into the community. This movement, which began in 1955 and accelerated between 1965 and 1985, reduced the state inmate hospital population by more than three-quarters.

Although deinstitutionalization was primarily motivated by economic factors,[304] its more idealistic adherents wrote, "By bringing the mentally ill back into the community, by enlisting the good will and the desire to serve, the ability to understand which is found in every neighborhood, we should meet the challenges that such groups of persons present, and at the same time ease the federal

---

304 See Anne Bradin Johnson, *Out of Bedlam: the Truth about Deinstitutionalization* (New York: Basic Books, 1990), p. 39, and Andrew Scull, *Decarceration: Community-Treatment and the Deviant* (New Brunswick, New Jersey: Rutgers University Press, 1993). Scull wrote deinstitutionalization was in response to "a broad expanse of social [federal welfare programs], growing fiscal pressures on the states, and the opportunity to transfer costs away from the state budget." Cited in Seth Farber, *Madness, Heresy and the Rumor of Angels*, p. 247.

burden of their confinement in fixed institutions."[305]

In reality, no attempt was made to integrate mental patients into the community. Deinstitutionalization was more aptly termed "trans-institutionalization" by Thomas Szasz. He wrote, "Deinstitutionalization was simply a new fashion in mental health care, consisting of storing unwanted persons in dwellings not called 'mental hospitals' but, nevertheless, treating them as if they were mental patients who required lifelong psychiatric supervision."[306]

From a more "moderate" viewpoint than Szasz, historian Andrew Scull came to the same conclusion: "It is only an illusion that patients who were placed in boarding or family care homes are in the community.... These facilities are for the most part like small long-term state hospital wards isolated from the community.... Little effort is directed toward social and vocational rehabilitation."[307] The only interaction former mental patients have is with their families (if they have families), who usually pressure their "sick" relative to comply with their psychiatrists, other mental patients, and mental health personnel who continually encourage them to accept their illness, and to take their "meds."

Although psychiatrists tout "anti-psychotic medication" as a miraculous breakthrough that makes it possible for the severely mentally ill to function, the fact is that these

305 Cited in Seth Farber, *Madness, Heresy and the Rumor of Angels: The Revolt Against the Mental Health System* (Chicago: Open Court Press, 1993), p. 246.

306 Thomas Szasz, *Cruel Compassion* (New York: John Wiley & Sons, 1994), p. 171.

307 Andrew Scull, *Decarceration: Community Treatment and the Deviant* (New Brunswick, New Jersey: Rutgers University Press, 1984). Cited in Seth Farber, *Madness, Heresy and the Rumor of Angels*, p. 247.

drugs are debilitating and destructive. Psychiatrist Peter Breggin has argued that the effects of these drugs are similar to that of a lobotomy: They cause a loss of initiative, a depression of motivation, blunting of emotions, and impairment of the patient's ability to reason and think abstractly.[308] In fact, the psychiatrists who introduced chlorpromazine (the first anti-psychotic or neuroleptic drug) to North America described it as "a pharmacological substitute for lobotomy."[309] (These drugs are highly addictive, and abrupt cessation will typically produce severe withdrawal effects.)

Psychiatrists in the early 1950s did not attempt to conceal the fact that it was precisely the lobotomy-like effects of the drugs that made them useful for them. British psychiatrist Peter Breggin wrote in 1954, "Patients responding well to the drug have developed an attitude of indifference both to their surroundings and their symptoms best summarized by the current phrase 'couldn't care less.'"[310]

A French psychologist wrote in 1956 "anti-psychotic medication" produced "a remarkable disinterest for all that had agitated the patient previously. In certain respects these drugs are comparable to stuporous phenomena....These phenomena are in intimate relation...to the therapeutic goal we were hoping to reach. That is why we busied ourselves to produce these states systematically by using and combining different drugs....Eventually we succeeded by continuous and combined medication with Chlorpromazine and Reserpine. Approximately half the patients...were

308 See Peter Breggin, *Psychiatric Drugs: Hazards to the Brain* (New York: Springer Publishing Co., 1983).
309 Cited in Ibid., p. 15.
310 Cited in Ibid., p. 15.

completely immobile. One could move them about like puppets....The other half of the patients also presented these phenomena, but in a less pronounced manner."[311] The psychiatrist closed his article by highly recommending the use of these drugs.

It is acknowledged by psychiatry today that these drugs produce severe neurological disorders in a majority of the patients who take them. These are said to be undesirable "side effects." A common disorder is *tardive dyskinesia* (TD), a frequently irreversible disease that usually begins with uncontrollable movements of the face, including the tongue, lips, mouth, and cheeks. The hands and feet and arms and legs can be involved. The movements include writhing contortions, tics, spasms, and tremors. Even mild cases are often grossly disfiguring and embarrassing to patients.

The American Psychiatric Association estimates that the prevalence rate of *tardive dyskinesia* in long-term users of neuroleptic drugs ranges from thirty to fifty-seven percent (virtually all of the former mental patients who remain in the mental health system).[312] Estimates of the number of individuals affected in America alone range from one-half million to several million.[313] It is by all accounts a

311 Cited in David Cohen, "Psychiatrogenics: Introducing Chlorpromazine in Psychiatry," in *Review of Existential Psychology and Psychiatry*, Volume XXIII, Nos. 1, 2, and 3, pp. 212-213.

312 "Tardive Dyskinesia, A Task Force Report of the American Psychiatric Association" (Washington, D.C.: American Psychiatric Association, 1992), pp. 63-64. This study also ruled out the possibility of causes of TD other than drug treatment.

313 Breggin, "Brain Damage, Dementia and Persistent Cognitive Dysfunction Associated with Neuroleptic Drugs," in David Cohen, ed., *Challenging the Therapeutic State*, p. 429.

widespread epidemic that Peter Breggin has called "possibly the worst medically-induced catastrophe in history."[314]

Akathisia is another frequent side effect of neuroleptics, occurring in an estimated forty-five percent of patients. *Akathisia* is extreme restlessness that often causes mental patients to pace back and forth. *Tardive dyskinesia* and *akathisia* are only two of the numerous side effects caused by neuroleptics.[315]

The side effects are destructive not only in and of themselves but also impede patients' recovery in a variety of ways. For example, their impact on cognition and motivation make it difficult, if not impossible, for patients to learn new skills, as a job would require. Cosmetically disfiguring *akathisia* and *tardive dyskinesia* "mark" individuals as "mental patients," thus making it more difficult for them to be reintegrated into the community. The side effects are usually viewed by the population as symptoms of mental illness.

The American Psychiatric Association continues to insist that neuroleptic drugs are the treatment of choice for schizophrenics, despite their side effects.[316] Psychiatrists frequently attribute the persistence of severe mental illness to the "irrational" reluctance of patients to consistently take their "medication." Peter Breggin has documented the highly financially lucrative and mutually rewarding relationship between the American Psychiatric Association

314 Ibid., p. 429.
315 See Peter Breggin, *Psychiatric Drugs: Hazards to the Brain.*
316 "Tardive Dyskinesia: A Task Force Report of the American Psychiatric Association," p. 244.

and the pharmaceutical companies.[317]

As I have shown in my book, all of the individuals who had "schizophrenic breakdowns" and fully recovered from them, going back to work or school, reintegrating themselves into the community, weaned themselves off psychiatric drugs, and extricated themselves from the mental health system. I have today spoken to several hundred individuals who have made the same accomplishment, thus belying psychiatric dogma that "mental illness" is "chronic" and intractable.

Furthermore, as David Cohen and Michael McCubbin noted, "Considerable evidence from controlled, random assignment studies clearly shows that *given the proper social environment*, most newly identified 'schizophrenics' can be treated successfully with little or no psychotropic medication."[318]

Despite their presence in our midst, "schizophrenics" and other former mental patients are relegated by psychiatrists to a caste of virtual untouchables, whose chances of social mobility are negligible and who exist in ghettos, supervised by mental health professionals and exiled from the community at large.

Psychosis as Baptism

Repeatedly St. Paul referred to the process of becoming a disciple of Christ as a death-rebirth experience. The new self arises from the ashes of the old. "For through the

317 Peter Breggin, *Toxic Psychiatry* (New York: St. Martin's Press, 1991), pp. 344-371.

318 David Cohen and Michael McCubbin, "The Political Economy of Tardive Dyskinesia," in D. Cohen, ed., *Challenging the Therapeutic State*, pp. 466-469.

law I died to the law so that I might live for God. I have been crucified with Christ and I no longer live, but Christ lives in me" (Galatians 2:19-20). In Ephesians 4:20-24, St. Paul wrote, "In reference to your former manner of life, you lay aside the old self, which is being corrupted in accordance with the lusts of deceit....Be renewed in the spirit of your mind, and put on the new self, which in the likeness of God is created in righteousness and the holiness of the truth."

Frequently the individual labelled "schizophrenic" is undergoing a severe personality crisis, a disintegration of the personality that makes possible the recreation of the self. This was first noted by R.D. Laing in *The Politics of Experience*: "Madness need not be all breakdown. It may also be breakthrough. It is potentially liberation and renewal as well as enslavement and existential death."[319] Although Laing eschewed Christian terminology in *The Politics of Experience*, his description is remarkably similar to that of St. Paul, "True sanity entails in one way or another the dissolution of the normal ego, that false self competently adjusted to our alienated social reality...and through this death a rebirth, and the eventual re-establishment of a new kind of ego-functioning, the ego now being the servant of the divine, no longer its betrayer."[320]

The disintegration of the self is frequently the precondition for the assumption of a new, more spiritually developed identity. It is the practices of the mental health system that convert the potential Christian initiate (or Buddhist initiate or shaman) into a chronic mental patient. This contention is further corroborated by anthropologi-

319 Laing, *The Politics of Experience*, p. 133.
320 Ibid., pp. 144-145.

cal data. In "Shamans and Acute Schizophrenia,"[321] Julian Silverman compared the initiatory ordeal typically experienced by the novice shaman to what psychiatrists term a "schizophrenic episode." He concludes, "Significant differences between acute schizophrenics and shamans are not found in the sequence of underlying psychological events which define their abnormal experience....One major difference is emphasized—a difference in the degree of cultural acceptance of a unique resolution of a basic life crisis. In primitive cultures in which such a unique life crisis resolution is tolerated, the abnormal experience (shamanism) is typically beneficial to the individual cognitively and affectively; the shaman is regarded as one with expanded consciousness. In a culture that does not provide referential guides for comprehending this kind of crisis experience, the individual 'schizophrenic' typically undergoes an intensification of the suffering over and above his initial anxieties."[322]

The investigation of shamanism is illuminating: Whereas personality disintegration was interpreted in premodern societies as the prelude to reintegration and as a sign that one was called upon to assume a leadership position in one's culture, in modern society it is interpreted as a symptom of a chronic disorder. The implications of this are staggering. Yesterday's shaman is today's chronic schizophrenic! The kind of person who, in a bygone era, would have been initiated into the vocation of shaman, medicine man, spiritual healer, is now likely to be initiated into the role of tragic-victim-of-the-most-serious-

321 Julian Silverman, "Shamans and Acute Schizophrenia," in *American Anthropologist,* 69, 1967, p. 21.
322 Ibid., p. 21.

mental-illness-known-to-modern-civilization.

The great philosopher of religion and student of shamanism Mircea Eliade also wrote that the disintegration of the personality was a precondition for the assumption of the new identity of the shaman: "The true knowledge, that which is conveyed by the myths and the symbols, is accessible only in the course of following upon the process of spiritual regeneration realized by initiatory death and resurrection....The future shaman, before becoming a wise man, must first know madness and go down into darkness."[323]

It is significant that six out of the seven individuals whose story I told during their breakdown not only had distressing or terrifying experiences but also had ecstatic and enlightening experiences of the kind described by mystics in the Christian tradition—as well as in other religious traditions. They perceived a mysterious order in the universe and felt the sense there was a benevolent higher power who was seeking to guide them—and us—through the dark night of the soul represented by modern civilization. Most of them experienced a sense of oneness with all beings (a common motif in Christian mysticism). None of them joined the Orthodox Church or any other Christian body, but they very well might have, had they encountered someone within the Church with a sympathetic ear.

The power of a breakdown to help an individual make a transition to a completely different mode of life is well illustrated, but the story I told in my previous book of a woman in her early twenties who changed her orientation

323 Mircea Eliade, *Myths, Dreams and Mysteries* (New York: Harper and Row, 1975), pp. 225-226.

from homosexual to heterosexual in a relatively brief period of time. Before her psychotic breakdowns, she had begun to believe that her homosexuality had become a façade that she felt compelled to maintain because of peer pressure. In her last psychotic episode, what was clearly at stake was her sense of personal identity. She told me, "I felt as if I was going to unravel to the point where there was no I." I speculated to myself that the sense of a future ripe with new possibilities caused and demanded this divestiture of self. This was analogous to the shamanic experience. Eliade has written, "The initiatory death repeats this exemplary return to chaos in order to make possible the renewal of the cosmogony; that is, to prepare for the new birth."[324] He notes that this often involves a total disintegration of the personality. In other words, my subject had undergone a kind of initiatory death as a transition to another mode of being. To use Eliade's words, she underwent "a trial indispensable to regeneration; that is, to the beginning of a new life."[325]

If we extrapolate from this data, it is clear that just as the disintegration of the personality, i.e., psychosis, was typically the precondition for becoming a shaman, so it could well be the initial phase—for many people, to one degree or another—in the death of our old self and the resurrection (note that Eliade uses the same term as St. Paul, see above, p. 13) of the new self formed in the likeness of Christ. Yet the individual experiencing a profound crisis of this kind who goes to a minister for help will invariably be referred to a mental health professional.

324 Mircea Eliade, *Myths, Dreams and Mysteries*, p. 224.
325 Ibid., p. 224.

What a terrible abdication of duty for Christians! At the moment of our greatest opportunity, when the individual is ready to make the transformation to a completely different mode of existence, to be reborn in the Spirit, we abandon them to mental health professionals, who above all else are determined to prevent this spiritual rebirth from occurring. If the Church is to become a vital force for social and spiritual transformation, She must reach out to individuals in their times of crisis.

The Church on the Line

It is the responsibility of the Church to incorporate mental patients into Her eschatological community—hopefully before they have become habituated to institutionalized lives. Patients' allegiance to the Church can only be *formal* as long as they remain spiritually and emotionally bonded to mental health professionals—a situation today sanctioned by the Church. This divorce must take place before they can become a functioning part of the Body of Christ. Otherwise they will remain professional mental patients, consciously and/or subconsciously seeking the approval of mental health professionals by conforming to their expectations (as indicated above in discussion on experimenter bias).

By integrating the "mentally ill" into the Christian community, the Church will belie the dogmas of the state-sponsored religion of psychiatric Science, affirm the worth and spiritual equality of all individuals, and demonstrate that the power of Christ is more effective in transforming human life than "professional expertise." A Church that includes the sane and the mad, former "mental patients"

and "normal" people, will belie the caste distinctions created by psychiatry that are today regarded by most people
as biological differences. Thus, like the early Church, which
included slaves and free individuals on an equal basis, it
will signify the birth of a new humanity. Herein lies its
truly evangelical significance.

PART FOUR

CHAPTER 11

St. Gregory of Nyssa

It is the thesis of this book that the solution to the debacle of civilization requires the recovery of an anthropology that is both Christian and humanistic. The antithesis posited by Augustinianism between God and humanity must be overcome in theory and in practice if Christianity is to be a force for cultural transformation. The Russian Orthodox philosopher S.L. Frank wrote approximately fifty years ago that "Christianity is the religion of worshipping God not as opposed but as deeply akin to man."[326] A Christian humanist anthropology could provide the philosophical foundation needed for the development of the capacity for love.[327]

Eastern Christian theology, Orthodoxy, has not been marred by the misanthropic premises that have been characteristic of Western Christian theology, Roman Catholic and Protestant, for centuries. From the early Greek fathers

326   S.L. Frank, *Reality and Man* (London: Faber and Faber, 1965), p. 123.

327   After completing this manuscript, I discovered *After Writing: On the Liturgical Consumation of Philosophy* by Catherine Pickstock (Oxford, U.K.: Blackwell, 1998), a profound and forceful Christian critique of post-modern philosophy. I was pleased to discover Ms. Pickstock's perspective is similar to my own (as it is developed in this last section) in that she seeks to affirm both the transcendence and the immanence of the divine. She brilliantly illuminates how secularist premises devolve into "the inevitably nihilistic conclusion of a rationalism indifferent to the specificities of human place, time, and desire" (p. 47).

ST. GREGORY OF NYSSA

to modern Orthodox theologians, one dominant theme has
been sounded again and again: the purpose of the Incarnation was to make it possible for human beings to be reunited with God, to become "partakers of the divine nature" (2 Peter 1:4). As St. Athanasius put it, "He (the Son of
God) became man, that we might become God."[328]

Western Christianity would have taken an entirely different course had it assimilated the teachings of the early
Greek Fathers instead of taking its lead primarily from
Augustine. For instance, we can only imagine the impact
on Western Christianity of St. Gregory of Nyssa, whom
Hans Urs von Balthasar described as "the most profound
Greek philosopher of the Christian era, an incomparable
mystic and poet,"[329] would have had if he, and not Augustine, was the major influence of Western Christendom.

In contrast to Augustine, St. Gregory denied (1) that
human nature is sinful, (2) that all human beings are
equally sinful, and (3) that humanity can do nothing but
sin. St. Gregory said human nature cannot be sinful, for
nature is what is created by God, and it was not created
evil or sinful. What is constitutive of our nature is that it is
created in the image of God. Christ is the image of God,
and man the image of Christ; man is the image of the Image.

Gregory's definition of God was succinct: "God by
His nature is goodness itself. Or rather, God transcends in
goodness everything that man can conceive or compre-
hend. Consequently He made human life from no other
impulse than because He is good....Man was made in God's

328 Cited in Constantine Tsirpanlis, *Introduction to Eastern
Patristic Thought* (Collegeville, Minnesota: Liturgical Press, 1991),
p. 66.

185

image. For this is like saying God made human nature a communicant of everything good." By saying that man was made in the image of God, it is implied that it is man's destiny, as Lossky put it, to participate "in the plenitude of the Divine Being, in the abundance of Divine Goodness."[330]

The source of evil lies in the freedom of man. Sin is not in the nature of humanity but is entirely an act of the will. Sin is sin because it is voluntary. Otherwise God would not condemn us for it.

Before the Fall, man existed in communion with God in a state of immortality.

> Then, death was not, disease was absent, "mine and thine"—these bad words—were far from the life of the First Man. For as the Sun is common to all and so is the air, and before all the grace of God and His blessing was common to all, so also in equal measure was participation in all good according to capacity open to all, the sickness of greed was unknown, the hatred of the superiors towards inferiors was not. (In fact there was no such thing at all as superiors.) And a thousand such other things which no one will ever be able to enumerate exhaustibly in words, and which man possessed in his greatness, I mean equality and honor to the angels, boldness of access into the presence of God, the vision of the super-cosmic good, and all the ineffable beauty of the Blessed Nature could then be seen in us also, manifesting the divine image

329 Cited in Paulos Mar Gregorios, *Cosmic Man* (New York: Paragon House, 1988), p. xvi.
330 Vladimir Lossky, *Orthodox Theology* (Crestwood, New York: St. Vladimir's Seminary Press, 1989), p. 124.

in themselves, in the prime of the soul when it was still shining.[331]

Once the commandment was broken by Adam and Eve, man was destined to die because he had abandoned God. "For sin is estrangement from God, who is the True and Only Life."[332] The Fall "shattered man's union with the angels"[333] and subjected humanity to an endless cycle of birth and death. This life, which most people today assume is natural, Gregory called a "life in death."[334] Death now casts its shadow over all existence, transforming the original state of ecstatic life into a "chilled life"[335] characterized by "sexual union, conception, birth, pollution, the nipple, food, excretion, gradual growth to full stature, adult life, sickness, death."[336]

Human nature is not evil, for it is God's creation. As St. Gregory puts it, "Human nature is still free to choose between good and evil, and that is the basis on which the call to repentance can be addressed to man."[337] For St. Gregory, needless to say, there is no division of humanity into an elect predestined to salvation and the larger mass predestined to damnation. Even the greatest sinners are summoned to return to God.

> For He said: "Return, oh sons of men." What is the teaching here? The word refers to the nature, and im-

331 Mar Gregorious, p. 183.
332 Ibid., p. 159.
333 Cited in Panayiotis Nellas, *Deification in Christ* (Crestwood, New York: St. Vladimir's Seminary Press, 1987), p. 53.
334 Ibid., p. 47.
335 Ibid., p. 48.
336 Ibid., p. 49.
337 Ibid., p. 164.

plies the healing from evil. For since being change-able you fell away from the good, you need again to be changing for the good....Thus it is in the choice of men to conduct themselves to that which they wish, either to the good or to the evil....For him who returns again to the good from his turning away, even if his life is spotted with myriad faults, the multitude of evils appearing together as a thousand years, when he turns to God it all becomes nothing...."[338]

Gregory does not accept the idea of irresistible grace. He writes, "Virtue compelled is not virtue."[339] In his theology and the teaching of the Orthodox Fathers, human effort complements the grace of God.

Although the image of God in man has been obscured by sin, it has not been destroyed or irreparably damaged. It is understandable, given the existence of evil, that some have come to this conclusion. St. Gregory notes, "Through those who have rightly ordered their lives, we can see the divine image in man. For someone who is carnal and a slave of passion makes it unbelievable that man was originally adorned with divine beauty, other persons who practice noble virtue and keep themselves pure from pollution should confirm you in the better conception of human nature."[340]

St. Gregory writes that since the Fall "the Godlike beauty of the soul which came into being an imitation of the archetype has been discolored like some iron implement by the rust of evil." And he urges his readers to wash this image by a pure way of life as if "with water" so that

338 *Cosmic Man*, p. 162.
339 Ibid., p. 210.
340 Ibid., p. 203.

"the beauty of the soul stands revealed once more."[341]

In the Orthodox Church, through the initiative of the Holy Spirit and the response of human beings, an eschatological process is taking place that will culminate in the gradual elimination of the consequences of evil. This process Gregory refers to as "passing through the fire of purification." Eventually there will be a universal restoration: "Participation in bliss awaits everyone....After many ages evil will disappear and nothing will remain except good. This will be the completion of the return of all intellectual creatures to the original state in which they were first created, when there was as yet no evil....The beauty of our similarity to God, in which we were formed at the beginning, will again shine forth."[342]

Contemporary Orthodox theologians agree with St. Gregory that salvation is a product of divine and human action, that the image of God has not been destroyed by the Fall; and they decisively reject the doctrine of predestination, affirming with Scripture that God desires the salvation of all. St. Gregory of Nyssa and the Orthodox tradition are at one with Western Christianity in their belief in a tragic Fall. Both traditions maintain that humanity's subjugation to disease, death, and sin are tragic consequences of the Fall. Where the traditions diverge radically is in their conception of the anthropological consequences of the Fall. Whereas Western theologians typically state that the Fall has partially or totally destroyed the image of God in man,

341 Cited in Gregory of Nyssa, *From Glory to Glory* (Crestwood, New York: St. Vladimir's Seminary Press, 1979), pp. 113-114.

342 Father Georges Florovsky, *The Eastern Fathers of the 4th Century* (Belmont, Massachusetts: Notable and Academic Books, 1987), p. 216.

Eastern theologians state that the image of God in man has been obscured by the Fall. The eschatological implications are obviously profoundly different. The doctrine of the destruction of the image of God coheres with the Augustinian idea of the bondage of the human will, and the dependence of human beings upon God for salvation. But if the image of God in man is merely obscured, then it lies within the power of those who become aware of the existence of the image—in however latent a state—to make it manifest once again and to summon others to the same task.

Twentieth century Orthodox theologian Father Georges Florovsky emphatically affirmed the indestructibility of the image of God in man. "Without doubt even in the demonic depths the creature remains the work of God and the traits of divine design are never effaced. The image of God, obscured by the infidelity of sin, is nevertheless preserved intact, and that is why there is always, even in the abyss, an ontological receptacle for divine appeal, for the grace of God."[343]

This is also why humanity retains the freedom and the responsibility to work—with the assistance of the grace of God—for the liberation of all humanity and for

343 Georges Florovsky, *Creation and Redemption*,(Belmont, Massachusetts: Nordland, 1976), p. 90. It is precisely because evil is a violation of human nature, not an expression of it, that we are offended by the immorality, cruelty, and injustice of human beings. Destructive acts by animals are not considered to be immoral or evil. As the Eastern Orthodox philosopher Phillip Sherrard wrote, "The ugliness of evil consists in the corruption of something that is essentially good. It is only because we are essentially good that we have the capacity for evil." Sherrard, *Human Image: World Image* (Ipswich, UK: Golgonooza Press, 1992), p. 172.

the reunion of all of creation with its divine Creator. "Our Lord left to us His own work to carry on and to accomplish. We have to enter into the very spirit of His redeeming work. And we are given power to do this. We are given power to be the sons of God."[344]

CHAPTER 12

The Limits of Secularism

St. Gregory of Nyssa, who lived in the same century as Augustine, articulated an ontology of plenitude, an interpretation of the Christian revelation at odds with those of his contemporaries who opted for Augustine's theory. Western Christianity theoretically could have taken a different path had it taken its bearing from St. Gregory and other church fathers whose intellectual acuity matched Augustine's but whose less jaundiced view of humanity enabled them to be faithful to the spirit of the Christian revelation.

If one locates the category of an ontology of plenitude on one end of a continuum, and the category of an ontology of deficiency at the other end, any ontology which is not fully sacramental inevitably moves, or slips, in the direction of the latter.

Sacramental ontology, in both its Christian and non-Christian versions, affirms both poles of the God-world axis. From this perspective a "secular" affirmation of the world that denies its bond with God is specious. The world cannot possess value in and of itself, but only by virtue of its bond with that which is infinitely valuable, holy. As Philip Sherrard noted, "Without the Divine—without God—there can be no holiness, nothing sacred."[345] Creation is sacred because God is "immanent" in it or, as St. Paul stated (perhaps more aptly), because we are in God

345 Philip Sherrard, *The Sacred in Art and Literature* (Ipswich, UK: Golgonooza Press, 1990), p. 1.

(Acts 17:28). Sherrard wrote, "Creation participates in the divine, and is an actual mode of existence or embodiment of the living, ever-present God."[346] Father Schmemann defines a sacramental ontology in almost identical terms: "The world...is an epiphany of God, a means of His revelation, presence, and power."[347]

Both Sherrard and the Russian Orthodox philosopher S.L. Frank critique the idea that the world exists outside of God. This is a typical misunderstanding of the biblical revelation that God created the world *ex nihilo*. This nothing cannot be a nothing that exists outside of God, because this would be that something exists outside of God from all eternity. The nothing out of which God creates is aptly described as "no-thing." It exists within God, as an aspect of his nature. It is "a ground of pure potentiality or receptivity at the heart of the divine, its innermost principle or pole."[348] This is the "feminine pole" of God, which complements the active and masculine principle of the divine nature: God as Creator. It is the "pre-ontological and pre-conscious abyss of infinite possibilities, the divine darkness, God's innermost ground."[349] This is the *nihil*, or non-being, out of which God brings creation into being.

S.L. Frank also argued that nothing cannot exist outside of God: "Every 'outside' as well as every within is posited by God Himself and is an element in His all-determining infinite fullness. Everything 'other than God' is 'other within God's own being'—it is 'God's other' or an

346 Sherrard, *The Eclipse of Man and Nature* (West Stockbridge, Massachusetts: Lindisfarne Press, 1987), p. 92.
347 Alexander Schmemann, *For the Life of the World* (Crestwood, New York: St. Vladimir's Seminary Press, 1988), p. 120.
348 *Christianity and Eros* (London: SPCK Press, 1976), p. 72.
349 Ibid.

element of otherness arising out of God's self unfolding."[350]
Sherrard and Frank are in agreement: Since there can be
nothing outside of God, He must create the world from
within Himself; thus it is within God that "we live, move
and have our being" (Acts: 17-28), although of course, God
in His infinitude transcends the world He has created.

A sacramental ontology overcomes the radical dualism of Augustinianism. It does not deem the world an obstacle to the union with God, nor does it not declare it an
illusion—as Hinduism does—which must be transcended
if we are to enter into communion with God. It maintains
that not merely the rites of the church but the entire realm
of creation, including nature and humanity, are sacraments
of God. The transcendent God "and the changing multi-
tudinous world of the senses constitute a single undivided
and indivisible reality."[351]

A failure to realize that the world is not independent
of God can take two forms: either the world is made an
object of idolatry and worshipped in itself, or its value is
disparaged or denied altogether. Both of these illusions
have led human beings to treat nature and other human
beings as objects to be used for materialistic ends. Only by
recovering a sense of the sacramental nature of creation
can we rekindle the natural sense of reverence and awe of
God's creation that will enable us to restore our communion with God and to fulfill our vocation as stewards of
creation.

The Augustinian antithesis between God and humanity manifests itself in secular humanism in an inverted

350 S.L. Frank, *Reality and Man* (London: Faber and Faber, 1965),
p. 17.
351 Philip Sherrard, *Human Image and World Image*, p. 32.

form. This may strike the reader as an egregious statement since secular humanism typically declares that there is no God, that God is dead. Man is a source of value, "God" is merely the fictitious creation of the baser instincts of human beings. Reading between the lines, one senses that the secularist is really convinced that if God does exist, we will have to abolish Him,[352] i.e., He constitutes a threat to the recognition of human dignity. Of course doubts about God's nonexistence are quickly dismissed; instead, the assertion is made that humanity is the source of all value. The dogmatism of secularism indicates that it remains haunted by the spectre of God.[353]

Father Schmemann argues that what is characteristic of secularism today is not the denial of the existence of God, but the denial that God's existence has any relevance for human beings other than in a realm that is specifically designated as religious. "The characteristic feature of the

352 René thinks that Nietsche has been misinterpreted. Nietsche argued not that God had died of "old age," that the notion of God is an anachronism that humanity has outgrown. His point seems to be that in an act of *hubris* human beings have attempted to replace God. Nietsche's famous quote from *The Gay Science* is rarely quoted in full. (This omission makes it more consistent with the conventional interpretation.) "God is dead. God remains dead. And we have killed Him. How shall we, the murderers of all murderers, comfort ourselves? What was holiest and most powerful of all that the world has yet owned bled to death under our eyes? Who will wipe His blood off us? What water is there for us to clean ourselves?" Cited in James G. Williams, ed., *The Girard Reader* (New York: Crossroad Publishing Co., 1996), pp. 256-257.

353 In fact, the baneful consequences of Augustinianism is at least one of the reasons for the original emergence of secular humanism; it must be acknowledged that in this regard it had, at least at an earlier point in time, a corrective effect on culture.

American culture and 'way of life' is that they simultaneously accept religion as something essential to man and
deny it as an integrated worldview shaping the totality of
human existence."[354]

For the American Christian, Roman Catholic and Protestant, acceptance of secularism is based on a profound
misunderstanding: Christ's purpose was not to found a
new religion but to inaugurate a new life. Secularism essentially asks us to live in the world as if there were no
God. But loyalty to the gospel and to the whole Christian
tradition "demands exactly the opposite: to live in the
world seeing everything in it as the revelation of God, a
sign of His presence, the joy of His coming, the call to communion with Him, the hope for fulfillment in Him."[355] Insofar as Christians fail to do this, they betray the Christian
faith.

354 Alexander Schmemann, *Great Lent* (Crestwood, New York:
St. Vladimir's Seminary Press, 1974), p. 108.
355 Schmemann, *For the Life of the World*, pp. 111-112.

CHAPTER 13

Christian Humanism: Beyond Secularism and Augustinianism

An account of an experience I underwent in 1984 while completing my dissertation may help clarify why I believe secularism is inadequate. As I was preparing the final chapter of my dissertation, a phenomenological study, I decided that for the sake of completeness I had to make a response to some of the metaphysical questions implicit in the material covered: Does life have meaning? Is it meaningful to speak of God?

During the two to three weeks that I worked on this chapter, I found myself engaging in an internal dialogue with one of the seven subjects of my study: "Oscar," a Unitarian minister in his early fifties, an atheist, and a long-term member of the American Humanist Association. Although in two interviews with me Oscar forcefully articulated a radical philosophy of moral and epistemological skepticism, he had been involved in a number of movements for social justice and humanitarian change, including the Civil Rights movement, the anti-Vietnam War movement, and various environmental causes.

Oscar first acknowledged that he felt these movements were "important," but when I pressed for further definition he reversed himself and stated that he believed that his own sense of importance was "merely subjective," and that he did not believe that there was an "ultimate

197

purpose" in the universe. He said that he thought that morality is relative (as evidenced by the fact that it differs from culture to culture), and he stated that there were no "absolutes." As a "rationalist," he believed that human beings' unwillingness to acknowledge these facts was a result of our tendency to choose comfortable illusions over unpleasant truths.

I felt some identification with Oscar, as I had been involved in many of the same movements and felt a commitment to the same causes. On the other hand, I found his worldview unappealing: I had spent much of the last ten years of my life studying mystics in various traditions (Christian, Hindu, Jewish, Buddhist), and although I did not identify with any particular tradition at that time, I strongly believed in God, and found that some of my most profound experiences occurred in the process of worshipping God—occasionally in a church or in a temple, but for the most part when I was alone, and most often when I was surrounded by "nature."

No sooner had I begun work on the conclusion and initiated my internal dialogue with Oscar, than I was plunged into the most profound crisis I had experienced since adolescence. As I remember, one incident marked the beginning of this period of confusion. I was having dinner with a friend. I felt tenderness for her and silently admired her delicacy of expression. But these feelings were nipped in the bud by the thought that—no, the vision, rather, of myself as an animal that was trying to endow its instinctual reactions with a sense of value, trying to feel important.

For over two weeks my ability to love and appreciate the world was stifled. Every time I would feel a reaction of love, appreciation, awe, or wonder, I would fear that I was deluding myself. The specter of meaninglessness made it virtually impossible for me to appreciate any person or event. Always the thought would intrude: I *am allowing myself to be deluded.* The bottom line was that I did not know. And I never could know. It was logically possible (at least), and would always remain so, that Oscar was right: that meaning was merely a subjective feeling. To affirm anything as meaningful seemed to be a betrayal of the truth.

I had lost the world I loved. My deep fear was that this loss would be permanent, that I would never regain the world I had lost. I would forever be plagued by this idea that Oscar might be right. I vacillated between despair and anxiety tinged with hope, engendered by the thought that there might be a solution. But there might not. Sometimes despite my distress I felt a sense of excitement, as if I was on a great adventure, as if I anticipated a miraculous providential solution to a dilemma that struck me as insoluble.

Through grace and effort I was gradually freed from the secularist demon. In the first place, after a few days I realized the obvious: that the appeal of Oscar's "rationalism" was entirely deceptive. Oscar claimed that he acknowledged no values, that he was free of illusions.

Yet I realized that even Oscar lived by a value: truth, reason. It was in the name of truth that he abjured all other values. But if he was consistent, he would acknowledge that reason/truth were themselves relative—tools that had only pragmatic value for biological beings engaged in a struggle for survival.

Oscar's position inevitably led, when thought through, to a profound state of confusion. Its seductiveness lay in its promise to liberate those who dared from the emotional fetters that bound the majority of weak human beings to their illusions, and to enable those courageous few to enter into the realm of truth shorn of all illusions. But if his premise was correct, then truth itself was merely another illusion!

If what we experience as valuable, e.g., beautiful, is merely an accidental result of a set of biological or chemical processes that just happened to have been initiated on our planet billions of years ago, then it is not *really* valuable—its apparent value is purely "subjective," illusory. If human life and values are essentially valuable then they cannot be the product of an accident. If meaning is the product of nonsense, then it is not really meaningful.

Every value or object exists within a horizon: the cause, the explanation, or the story of its genesis and existence. Its horizon constitutes its essence. If its essence is different from its appearance—how it seems to us—then the latter is *ipso facto* false, a delusional product of our subjectivity.

Typically, secularists are convinced that life is a product of random genetic mutations maintained by nature because they were conducive to the biological survival of a species. *Thus the universe has no objective value,* and secularists, insofar as they are consistent, cannot genuinely affirm the meaningfulness of life. They cannot love fully, for their surrender to the feelings of love or reverence must be checked by the thought that the object of these feelings is really *worthless.*

Thus, my own process of internal questioning and questing led me to the conclusion that in order to vouchsafe the value of the world we must affirm the existence of

God, of an infinite being who is *ipso facto* without horizons, and who is the explanation for the meaning of the universe that He has Himself created—the alternative is a self-refuting relativism.

Yet, I was still troubled by the idea that the universe might not really matter, that our existence was not of absolute importance. I asked myself, Why did God create the universe? Is our existence a matter of divine caprice or whim? Is it an arbitrary expression of God's will? Is it an accident? And if it is not an accident, what is it? I wrote, "What could God's justification possibly be? Is it that God has no justification? Here we reach the limits of the mind; it is as if it is poised over an abyss of meaninglessness, of absurdity."

The typical theistic explanation for human existence is more convincing to me than the secularist, but here, too, the threat of human existence subsumed under the rubric of an accident cast an ominous shadow. However, I reasoned, *the world makes sense.* "The very possibility of communication is proof of this, this is certain to me now....Therefore, it cannot be an accident that sense—meaning—exists. For that is to say that sense is a product of nonsense, that its own horizon contradicts it....It is no accident that we exist, that truth exists, that love exists."

In my search for a coherent narrative explanation for existence, the best I could think of was that God created the world for mysterious reasons that lie beyond the grasp of the mind; nonetheless, this was sufficient at the time to banish my fears that the world was suspended in an abyss of meaninglessness.

Approximately ten years later I discovered several books written by Philip Sherrard. The mistake in the traditional theistic view, Sherrard argued, lies in the premise that God "could quite as well have chosen not to create it (the world) as to create it."[356] If this were the case, it would mean that "creation is in no way necessary to God's self-fulfillment."[357] But what is not a necessary consequence of God's being what He is, is "something adventitious, gratuitous, and even a kind of appendage."[358] The problem with this account is that it evokes the image of a hiatus—of a rupture—between God and creation, between the infinite and the finite. Thus, it suffered from the same kind of dualism that afflicts Augustinianism and secularism, although in a more attenuated manner.

But does not Sherrard's assertion that God had to create the world entail that God is not free? No, because God is not compelled by any force external to Himself to create the world but by the "inner compulsion" every being has to fulfill its own nature.[359] Sherrard explains, "It is in accordance with this compulsion from within—with this necessity for self-determination—that God acts when He creates the world....It is an act in which absolute freedom and absolute necessity coincide...."[360]

Our existence is not accidental: It had to be. God must love, and God must create: "The reality of love is a property inherent in the essence of the lover...the Divine Lover—God—cannot not love at all or love to a limited extent, or not extend His love to the furthest limits of possibility and

356   Philip Sherrard, *Human Image, World Image*, p. 156.
357   Ibid., p. 156.
358   Ibid., p. 157.
359   Philip Sherrard, "Creation as Eucharist," *Epiphany Journal*, Volume 13, No. 3, Spring 1993, p. 43.
360   Ibid., p. 43.

so abstain from loving fully. He does not have that choice."[361]

The same holds for creation. "Creation is intrinsic to God's very life, it is the inner landscape of His own being, God making Himself visible to Himself and simultaneously making Himself visible to us. It is in some sense His very self." [362]

No account can completely explain the mystery of the relationship of the Infinite to the finite, of God to man. But a coherent narrative account—speculative metaphysics couched in the language of myth—will evoke the recognition of the psyche and bring the intellect and intuition into harmonious resonance. It does not dispel the mystery but illuminates it in such a way that as we look through the glass we do not see quite so darkly as we did before. This is the accomplishment of the narrative Sherrard has adumbrated, in which God not only creates the world but is bonded to it as a manifestation of His own transcendent essence.

Worship as Mode of Knowing and Being

Secularism arbitrarily privileges one *particular* mode of inquiry: natural scientific investigation. It not only excludes the revelations of religious traditions, but the revelations of mystics throughout the centuries, and of contemporary human experience. It denies that love (worshipping, wondering, marveling, etc.) can itself be a mode of cognition. But if the object of inquiry is sacred or divine,

361 Sherrard, *Human Image, World Image*, p. 157.
362 Ibid., p. 157.

then there can be no genuine knowledge without love, without worship.

Schmemann states that it is only in worship that human beings can attain true knowledge of the world as well as knowledge of and communion with God. He writes of worship that: "Being knowledge of God, it is the ultimate fulfillment of all human knowledge."[363]

It is an axiom of the Christian faith that we know God through worship. As Eastern Orthodox philosopher Paul Evdokomiv wrote, "We prove God's existence by worshipping Him and not by advancing so-called proofs. We have here the liturgical and iconographic argument for the existence of God. We arrive at a solid belief in the existence of God through a leap over what seems true, over the Pascalian certitude. According to an ancient monastic saying, 'Give your blood and receive the Spirit.'"[364]

By the time I finished the final chapter in my dissertation, I realized that secularism's quarrel was not merely with religion—it was with life itself. For the *appreciation* of life is already instinctively religious, an attitude toward the world, an orientation, an act of submission to that which is felt to be greater than oneself, to the objective goodness and beauty the world's qualities manifest. Worship,[365] I concluded—affirming the infinite holiness of God

363 Alexander Schmemann, *For the Life of the World* (Crestwood, New York: St. Vladimir's Seminary Press, 1973), pp. 120-121.

364 Paul Evdokimov, *The Art of the Icon: A Theology of Beauty* (Redondo Beach, California: Oakwood Publications, 1972), p. 23.

365 Eastern Orthodoxy in its liturgy succinctly defined worship: "It is meet and right to sing of Thee, to bless Thee, to praise Thee, to give thanks to Thee, and to worship Thee in every place of Thy dominion." Cited in Schmemann, *For the Life of the World*, p. 118.

and giving thanks for the life that He has granted to us—is the completion of the spontaneous movement that begins with the recognition of life as valuable.

The secularist will not worship. He regards any ritual affirmation of life as a betrayal of reason or a capitulation to superstition. And so, his surrender to life is not complete, cannot be completed. It is as if one were to have a love affair and never say, "I love you." The lover might act generously, lovingly, selflessly, but something would be missing. The secularist may be committed to life, but she is unwilling to affirm this commitment.

By separating the world from God, secularism causes a split in our own being—for we are essentially worshipping beings. In other words, secularism results in a diminishment in the sense of being, and prevents one from realizing the natural depth that life possesses when it is conscious of its own roots in the infinite, in God.

In their own respective ways, both secularism and Augustinianism represent a Promethean revolt against the conditions of creaturely existence. Secularism accepts human beings' appreciation of creation, but seeks to prevent the gesture of thanksgiving that points beyond creation to that which it symbolizes, to its transcendent source, to its infinite ground, to the Transcendent God. Augustinianism denies the world as a means of God's revelation, refuses to accepts God's immanence in creation, and affirms *only* His transcendence. One denies God, the other denies creation. In both cases there is the denial of the sacramental dimension of human existence—which results in an impoverishment of the ability to love. Orthodox sacramentalism affirms that there is no antithesis, no gulf between creation and God; to affirm one at the expense of the other is to alienate oneself from both.

Christian Humanism

Sacramentalism does not deny that human beings have a special role to play within creation. The sacredness of the world reaches conscious awareness only in man. In that sense there *is* a hiatus between God and nature. But it is bridged by the human being, the ambassador of the divine in the world of nature, by the priest of God who gives voice to the silent holiness of being.

Philip Sherrard states that worship is the means of effecting what he calls the "nuptial union between God and nature." "It is in and through us that the physical world is hallowed and that its intrinsic sacramental quality is revealed. It is we who are the priests of the temple of this world."[366] It is this understanding of the human vocation, as the priests of creation, that is the basis for Eastern Christian (Orthodox) humanism.

Alexander Schmemann also argues that man's dominion over creation is fulfilled in priesthood. He holds this power by *sanctifying* the world, by "making" it into communion with God.[367] By gratitude and adoration the created world is transformed by human beings into a spiritual world that reflects God's presence. "The first, the basic definition of man is that he is *the priest* (emphasis in original). He stands in the center of the world and unifies

366 Philip Sherrard, *The Sacred in Art and Literature* (Ipswich, U.K.: Golgonooza Press, 1990), p. 12.

367 Alexander Schmemann, *Of Water and the Spirit* (Crestwood, New York: St. Vladimir's Seminary Press, 1974), pp. 95-96.

it in his act of blessing God, of both receiving the world from God and offering it to God—and by filling the world with this eucharist, he transforms his life, the one he receives from the world, into life in God, into communion with Him."[368]

From this point of view all human beings, not merely the clergy, are called to be priests, to consecrate creation.[369] It should be noted that those who are deemed "mentally ill" are not exempted. In fact, one of the reasons for their emotional distress may be that they have difficulty adjusting to a world in which they are not invited to exercise their own functions as priests of God. The Orthodox Christian view stands in stark contrast with the Augustinian view that human beings are inherently depraved, with the Freudian view that human beings are naturally and essentially pathological, and with the assumption underlying biological psychiatry that a human being is a functional or dysfunctional biochemical machine.

The Christian humanism of the Eastern, Orthodox Church is antithetical to modern psychology, as well as to classical Augustinianism in both its Roman Catholic and Protestant forms. Modern psychologists frequently blame many of the problems of modern life on "low self-esteem." Christians frequently respond to this by claiming that we are called upon to esteem only God, not ourselves. This is an Augustinian response, not a Christian response, as it sets up a false opposition, which is countered by the sac-

368 Alexander Schmemann, *For the Life of the World*, p. 15.
369 We will not discuss here the justifications for having a specialized group of clergy.

ramentalist perspective. The issue is not *either* God or humanity but *both* God and humanity.

Secularists, on the other hand, do not understand that it is impossible to truly esteem human beings while denying our relationship to God and positing that a human being is essentially a natural creature seeking to fulfill biologically determined needs, "merely a neutral specimen of created natural being."[370] Instead, dignity is imparted to us by God and by the fact that "man is the creature in and through which God seeks to express *His own nature as spirit, personality, and holiness*."[371] "The One who called you is holy: like Him, be holy in all your behavior, for scripture says, 'You shall be holy, for I am holy' " (1 Peter 1:15-16, citing Leviticus 19:2).

Many Christians influenced by Augustinianism fail to understand that it is impossible to truly reverence God without reverencing humanity. We do not do honor to the artist by praising his personality and denigrating his creation. Because human beings have the potential for holiness, because we bear the image of God within ourselves, because as priests of God we are called upon to bring God's work to completion and to transform nature into a temple of enduring praise—because of all this, genuine reverence for God requires reverence for humanity.

But, perhaps above all, it is because Christ is the model for our humanity—as Christian revelation makes clear—that Christianity provides a basis not for the denigration

370 S.L. Frank, *Reality and Man* (London: Faber and Faber, 1965), p. 122.
371 Ibid., p. 220.

of humanity but for the fullest affirmation—for a profound humanism.[372]

372 Karl Barth wrote later in his life, "To find the true and essential nature of man we have to look not at Adam, the fallen man, but to Christ, in whom what has been fallen has been cancelled and what was original has been restored." Cited in Robin Scroggs, *The Last Adam* (Philadelphia, Pennsylvania: Fortress Press, 1966), p. 101. Sherrard agrees; he wrote, "Christ is the model of our humanity." Sherrard, *The Eclipse of Man and Nature* (West Stockbridge, Massachusetts: Lindsfarne Press, 1987), p. 43.

CHAPTER 14

The Christian
Developmental Model

The growth model I have described in previous chapters was characterized in general terms that are neither Christian nor explicitly sacramentalist (although it is compatible with sacramentalism). The growth model holds that each individual in the course of maturation experiences "problems in living." Emotions that the individual feels when contending with these problems (e.g., anxiety, despair) are not "symptoms of mental illness" but integral concomitants of the process of growth. All of the phenomena currently subsumed under the mental disease model can more adequately be explained and resolved by interpreting them through the categories of the growth model.

Let me give another example here. While I was working on my post-doctoral internship in 1986 (in an "outpatient clinic" in a lower-income area in New York City) I became increasingly aware of how degrading and destructive the medical model was to clients. The question I was grappling with was, Why did only very few individuals "see through it?" It is accepted not only by the overwhelming majority of mental health professionals but even by intellectuals and artists who one would expect to be more critical of the received wisdom of the time.

Alasdair Macintyre provides a solution. In surveying contemporary revolutions in philosophy and science, he wisely noted, "When an epistemological crisis is resolved, it is by the construction of a new narrative which enables the agent to understand *both* how he or she could intelligibly have held his or her original beliefs *and* how he or she could have been so drastically misled by them. The narrative in terms of which he or she at first understood an ordered experience is itself made into the subject of an enlarged narrative."[373]

I had two explanations—besides the obvious vested economic and status interests of professionals—for the persistence of the disease model. In the first place, it is familiar: It is continuous with the older ontology of deficiency that has stifled the spiritual growth of Western civilization for centuries. In Jungian terms, we might say that the collective unconscious of humanity is enthralled by the archetype of flaw, mesmerized by the Augustinian *mythos* of the incurable deformation of human nature, the legacy of the culture of sin and guilt that tormented humanity for centuries.[374]

A second explanation for the apparent intelligibility of the concept of mental illness is the fact that both the physician on the one hand, and the psychotherapist and the educator on the other hand, deal with situations in which there is a disparity between the actual state that persons are in and an ideal or desired state that they imagine and desire. When psychiatrists are consulted by troubled patients, they need a rationale for intervention, and as physicians the most appealing one is that the patient is suffering from a mental illness that needs to be treated. The common feature underlying illness and

373 Seth Farber, "Transcending Medicalism," *The Journal of Mind and Behavior,* Vol. 8, No. 1, Winter, 1987), p. 107.

374 Jean Delumeau, *Sin and Fear: The Emergence of a Western Guilt Culture; 13th-19th Century* (New York: St. Martin's Press, 1990).

growth—a disparity between the actual and the ideal—helps to explain why intelligent people have systematically over centuries misclassified therapeutic and educational challenges as medical problems or illnesses.

Virtually all of the clients that consulted me were frightened that there was "something wrong" with them. The other mental health professionals they consulted consistently confirmed their fears, thus compounding their problems. By the fourth or fifth month of my internship, I had decisively rejected the medical model. I adapted a stance of what I termed "metaphysical all-rightness" and attempted to convey to my clients that there was nothing wrong with them. Since virtually every problem a client ever presented to me could be viewed as a challenge to them to become wiser or more competent in some area of their life, there was no need to construe the existence of their problem as evidence of deficiency.

By utilizing a growth model, I was drawing upon the cultural values ascribed to process of growth that are positive, rather than negative, as in illness. Compare, for example, the difference between a physician treating a patient for cancer, and parents coaching their infant toddler to walk. There was a time in a distant epoch when children were essentially viewed as deficient adults;[375] but childhood is now regarded as a natural state, and children are regarded as whole beings who are simply not grown-up.[376]

375 See John Sommerville, *The Rise and Fall of Childhood* (Beverly Hills, California: Sage Publications, 1982), pp. 47-49, and Philippe Ariès, *Centuries of Childhood* (New York: Vintage Books, 1962).

376 I'm not arguing that physical illness should be redefined as growth, but rather that the phenomenon termed "mental illness" is

The process of nurturing and educating children is not treated as an onerous burden parents and teachers are forced to bear. In this culture, we do not regard the fact that children have many obstacles to overcome in the course of their development as an occasion for pity, disgust, and pathos (the feelings that mental health professionals experience when dealing with "the mentally ill"). Typically parents and teachers—or at least "good" parents and "good" teachers—look upon their children or students with reverence and exalt in every triumph of the child over the challenges that life presents (the first words spoken, the first steps taken, graduation from kindergarten, as so forth).[377]

The contrast between the growth model and the disease model may be most marked in terms of children, but it is also apparent with young adults who are, for example, attending school, or even adults who have returned to school. Even the most talented student is not expected to have the competence of a seasoned scholar. The process of nurturing and educating children and young people is one from which adults derive a sense of meaning and purposefulness.

In 1985, as a result of my studies in family therapy, I came increasingly to rely upon it as a modality for helping individuals to solve their problems, which were usually interpersonal in nature. But in more general philosophical

vastly different, that the resolution of these problems is impeded by the theories and practices of mental health professionals.

[377] The reverence with which children are held in this culture (they are frequently described as "precious") may be said to be implicitly, if not explicitly, sacramental. They are often treated (as adults rarely are) as icons of God who manifest His purity and innocence.

terms, I based these interventions on a growth model that posited that each person is involved in a natural and idio-syncratic[378] process of emotional, intellectual, and spiritual maturation that—with appropriate support and guidance (not necessarily from a therapist)—leads to an increasing mastery of the challenges of life and an enhanced ability to live in harmony with the environment.

The growth model is not based on a naiveté about human behavior or an ignorance about the depth and ex-tent of human suffering. (Neither a medical model nor a growth model in themselves can adequately explain the existence of demonic evil, displayed in the likes of Charles Manson or Joseph Stalin.) This model can accommodate the fact that individuals frequently act in ways that are not conducive to their own emotional and spiritual well-being and development. (They do this as a result of igno-rance, anxiety, confusion, and/or habit.) It is not that they are mentally ill or defective; they simply do not possess the wisdom, skills, and/or trust in the environment that would enable them to resolve by themselves the particu-lar life challenges that confront them as individuals. The role of the therapist as I saw it then was not to eradicate an illness but to provide guidance, direction, and emotional support to persons who are involved in a natural process of learning and growth. (As I see it now, this is—with theo-logical modifications—the role of the Church.)

Once I had abandoned the medical model my efficacy as a therapist increased dramatically. To give one illustra-tion, toward the end of my post-doctoral internship in 1985,

378 By idiosyncratic, I mean that the process of growth has fea-tures unique to the individual that cannot be predicted by placing the individual in a general category, as in psychiatric diagnosis.

THE CHRISTIAN DEVELOPMENTAL MODEL

I was consulted by a client named Adam who had been diagnosed by the psychiatrist in the clinic as having a "major depression" and "an avoidant personality disorder." He was twenty-two years old and had just transferred to a school in New York City (where he grew up) after having spent several years in a college in Pennsylvania. In Pennsylvania he had had a number of friends in school and had felt very much at home. Now he was lonely, felt uncomfortable in social situations, and had no friends. This was a source, not only of boredom and loneliness, but of consternation, because he was afraid that there was something "wrong with him," that he was somehow defective or "mentally ill."

Had he been seen by any of the therapists in the clinic other than myself, he would have been referred back to the psychiatrist, who would have placed him on antidepressant medication and he would have attended therapy at least twice a week for months, if not years, to determine the source of his depression and of his personality disorder. I reassured him that there was nothing wrong with him. I reinterpreted his problem from a symptom of a mental disorder to a lack of experience, social skills, and "shyness." I said to him, "Social skills come with practice. You tend to be shy, you have more difficulty making friends in the beginning. But the fact that you had a number of friends in Pennsylvania proves that you can do so again." Since he seemed reluctant at first to initiate any moves toward making more friends, I "prescribed the symptoms": I suggested that he make no efforts to make friends, that this would happen naturally when the time was right and he was ready.

Within three weeks his depression had dissipated

completely. When I asked him how he accounted for the disappearance of his depression, he responded that my remarks helped him to realize that there was really "nothing wrong" with him. We agreed to reduce the therapy sessions from once weekly to once every two weeks—this move seemed to further bolster his self-confidence. After several months, he spontaneously and rather effortlessly made several friends. We agreed to terminate therapy, a move that infuriated my supervisor (a psychologist), who insisted that the diagnosis proved that Adam was seriously mentally ill and needed long-term therapy and medication. The tension between us was so great that I terminated my internship at that time, two months prematurely. (I did a "follow-up" on Adam, approximately six months later, and he reported that he had several friends at school and was happy with his life.)

I have described my interactions with Adam not because they were particularly challenging, or because his story was unusually fascinating. The point is that it starkly illustrates the "therapeutic value" of *merely* communicating to individuals confidence in their competence and spiritual integrity. I did not see this "client" for more than twelve sessions, and yet the problem was entirely resolved simply by conveying to him that there was nothing wrong with him.

Unlike the mental illness model, which demeans individuals, the growth model encourages them. It is frequently implicitly, if not explicitly, sacramental, as we saw above when considering the case of children.[379] It is in stark contradiction to conventional psychiatric classification, as brought out by Szasz' poignant observation:

379 See Footnote 5 above.

The vocabulary of psychiatric diagnosis is in fact a massive pseudo-medical justificatory rhetoric of rejection.... Being considered or labelled mentally disordered—abnormal, crazy, mad, psychotic, sick, it matters not what variant is used—is the most profoundly discrediting classification that can be imposed on a person today. Mental illness casts the "patient" out of our social order just as surely as heresy casts the "witch" out of Medieval society.[380]

If a growth model were adopted in the mental health field, it would revolutionize the field within a few years. Such a model threatens the status of mental health professionals, it undermines the caste system they have created, it will put psychiatrists and many other mental health professionals out of business as custodians of those deemed "the chronically mentally ill," and it will significantly reduce the demand for mental health professionals, resulting in a massive loss of jobs and income. That is why the growth model has no future within the mental health system—even though in a ten-year period it could save millions of persons from spiritual and/or physical devastation or destruction.

The Christian Model

The growth model, despite its advantages, is limited and insufficient from a Christian perspective. In the first place, in its secular form it does not explicate that the basis for love is our creation in the image of God, and that full spiritual maturity cannot be attained independently

380 Thomas Szasz, *The Manufacture of Madness* (New York: Harper and Row, 1970), p. 237.

of communion with God. Furthermore, this model in its secular form assumes that the world in which we live is natural, that the "human condition" is inexorable, governed by laws of nature. From a Christian perspective the "human condition" is a purely contingent manifestation of our estrangement from God and from each other, a symptom of our fallen state.[381]

We tend to take for granted the "laws of nature," forgetting that what we call "health" is really an ephemeral accord between the individual and nature, both of which are subjected to the dominion of death. This perspective is articulated most forcefully by the early Greek Fathers and by a number of modern Orthodox theologians: Physical death is not a natural phenomenon, but the abnormal result of our estrangement from God. St. Athanasius described the Fall as a product of man's decision to separate himself from God, to break the abiding communion between creature and Creator. Florovsky terms it "a kind of delirium, a self-erotic obsession, a spiritual narcissism."[382] The human being is the channel of grace for all of creation; our apostasy estranges all of nature from God and "shatters the cosmic harmony,"[383] leading to a "disorganization of the entire structure of being."[384] Death is not ordained by God but is "a deep tragedy, a painful metaphysical catastrophe"[385] that casts a shadow over all existence.

381 See Chapter 3 above.
382 Georges Florovsky, *Creation and Redemption* (Belmont, Massachusetts: Norland Press, 1967), p. 85.
383 Ibid., p. 106.
384 Ibid., p. 84.
385 Ibid., p. 105.

But since man's soul is rooted in God, the estrangement cannot be complete. S.L. Frank, the Russian Orthodox philosopher, states that it is a "weakening or attenuation" of man's connection to God, yet so radical that man no longer experiences communion with God.[386] Sherrard describes it as the self's denial of the soul, a spiritual murder, which brings the individual under the power of demonic forces.[387]

Yet it turns out on closer examination that this abnormal state is more aptly termed a crisis than an illness: There is not a complete breach of nature. The Greek Fathers tell us, for example, that Adam and Eve were created imperfect and had to be tested as free beings, and to become perfect through the stages of growth and maturity.[388] Thus the Patristic Christian model is a growth model that views nature as aiding human beings, making possible their fullest spiritual maturation. The stage we are at today is one of crisis, which we can resolve only by moving ahead. In other words, *as catastrophic as the consequences of the Fall were, in a sense it was necessary in order for humanity to progress to a higher stage of development where it would again choose to enter into communion with God.*

The great Christian philosopher Nikolai Berdyaev put it well in the 1930s: "The innocence imposed in paradise could not be maintained; it had no value and we cannot return to it. Men in the world are undergoing a voluntary testing, in the experience of the freedom of knowledge,

---

386   S.L. Frank, *Reality and Man*, p. 179.
387   Sherrard, *The Eclipse of Man and Nature*, pp. 30-31.
388   Constantine Tsirpanlis, *Introduction to Eastern Patristic Thought and Orthodox Theology* (Collegeville, Minnesota: Liturgical Press, 1991), p. 47.

and they must turn freely to God and to His Kingdom....Human personality does not awaken from the state
of unconsciousness produced by the Fall, and separation
from God except by a long and very painful struggle and
growth."[389] Redemption is thus not merely a return to paradise but "a new moment of creation."[390] *Both* Berdyaev and
Staniloae described it as "the return of the prodigal son,"
and Staniloae noted "the return of the prodigal son is the
return of the son matured through experience, and the
meeting of father and son is marked by a much more profound manifestation of parental love...."[391]

The individual's growth within the parameters of this
world is intrinsically limited. It is growth within a world
that is estranged from God, a world where each individual
regards his neighbor as his competitor, his enemy, a world
under the dominion of death.

Thus, in order to provide optimal conditions for each
individual's happiness and growth, humanity must solve
its developmental crisis, it must take a leap forward. As
Christians, our hope that this is possible is nourished by
our conviction that we are enabled in this task by Father,
Son, and the Holy Spirit. We all—whether we are labelled
"mentally ill" or not—face the same existential plight, the
universal human dilemma. We are all exiles, prodigal sons
and daughters, yearning for the day when we will return
to our homeland, the day of the Lord.

Another limitation of secularism is that it posits that
nature is autonomous, that it is self-sufficient: In other

389 Nicolai Berdyaev, *Freedom and the Spirit*, p. 186, p. 224.
390 Ibid., p. 178.
391 Dumitru Staniloae, *Theology and the Church* (Crestwood, New
York: St. Vladimir's Seminary Press, 1980), p. 171.

words, it fosters an illusion that prevents us from recognizing the sacramental nature of creation and thus affirming and *actualizing* the holiness of creation, of realizing the immanence of God in creation. Even in the fallen world, disfigured by death, nature remains an epiphany of God. If we fail to realize this, the development of our capacity for love will be stunted, and love will not attain to its natural depth—which is infinite. Thus, secularism prevents human beings from fulfilling the divine task of reuniting all of the created order with God.

Augustinianism Versus Christianity

I want to call the reader's attention to the contrast between the premises of Christian theology articulated in this chapter and that of Augustine. (See chapters 1 to 3.) The intrinsic worth of the soul has not been diminished by the Fall. The image of God in man remains intact. But it has been obscured, thus leading us to act in such a manner that we fail to fulfill our vocations as stewards of creation, as priests of God. Although we have free will, our ignorance of who we are imperils our existence. As Sherrard wrote, "Unless we become conscious of our inherent nobility, as well as that of every other existing thing, we are not likely to be stirred to make even the slightest gesture capable of initiating a movement of thought and action toward the recovery of our lost spiritual vision and being."[392]

Second, the human situation does not appear to be what was originally intended by God. We now live in a fallen world characterized by death, suffering, and perva-

392 Philip Sherrard, *Human Image, World Image*, p. 173.

sive evil. However, the Fall is not adequately interpreted either as a senseless mistake or as a nefarious crime. It was a necessary and inevitable expression of humanity's lack of spiritual maturity. The innocent love between God and man lacked the depth of a love that has passed through the trials of experience. Thus, our estrangement from God was in some sense inevitable for our growth to maturity. Only in the (relative) void of God's absence could we come to appreciate the significance of what had been lost. Only in that void could love become conscious of itself and thus mature.

Accepting that the Fall was necessary for our spiritual evolution releases us from the bondage to the past, from feelings of guilt and deficiency, and from the chains of regret. Accepting the finality of the past, of all that has gone before, allows us to be fully receptive to the promises of the future. This is imperative, because the consequence of the Fall has been a developmental crisis for the species that has lasted for centuries and that now has reached catastrophic proportions. The future confronts us as God's coworkers with the task of resolving this crisis, and of working to create the conditions for the Kingdom of God on earth.

Third, all of humanity is offered the gift of salvation. The assumption that some or many are predestined to eternal torment leads human beings either to adopt an attitude of misanthropic elitism (if they deem themselves among the elect), or of shame and of terror (if they count themselves among the damned), which creates an artificial division within humanity that makes it impossible to act with the spirit of unity that is prerequisite for our salvation.

Fourth, as I have emphasized repeatedly throughout these pages, we cannot cogently affirm the transcendence of God without affirming at the same time the derivative holiness of man, nor can we intelligibly affirm the holiness of man without affirming also the transcendence of God. God is both immanent in creation and transcendent of it.

Those who adopt the perspective of Christian humanism are not burdened by a sense of ontological deficiency and total depravity. We are aware of the tragic nature of fallen existence, and adhere to the general position of Eastern Orthodoxy, and to many Roman Catholics and Protestants, that it is our responsibility to participate with God in the process of redemption. We remember that Christ has admonished us to love one another as He has loved us, and He believed that it was in our power as human beings to do works that were greater than His own. As we listen to the groaning of the whole creation, we are aware that it is within our power—if we so choose—working with the grace of God, to alleviate the suffering that abounds in the universe and to create the preconditions for the final inbreaking of the Kingdom of Heaven on earth.

The Church as the Agent of God's Kingdom

From a Christian point of view, we can attain to full maturity only within the Church. It is here that we can attain "to the whole measure of the fullness of Christ" (Ephesians 4:13). It is here that we can overcome the divisiveness that manifests itself in human domination and violence. "We will in all things grow up into Him who is the Head, that is Christ. From Him the whole body, joined and held together by every supporting ligament, grows and builds itself up in love, as each part does its work" (Ephesians 4:15-16). As the Church provides the culture in which the individual can grow spiritually, the spiritual growth of the individual contributes to the growth of the Church as an organism—the process is dialectical.

As this point questions arise. I have asserted that man is essentially a worshipping being. But worship does not take place only in the Church. Does this not demonstrate then that one can lead a sacramental life outside of the Church? Is the Church indispensable for fostering human beings' spiritual growth? Furthermore, what is distinctively Christian about the sacramentalist perspective?

To answer these questions I think we must first identify the essential nature and purpose of the Church: to continue the messianic work of Christ, to transform the world, to create the conditions for the realization of the Kingdom of God on earth. Short of this transformation we will never be able to fulfill Christ's commandment to love one another as He has loved us. One of the ways in which the Church serves its messianic function is by creating a culture in which worship becomes a way of life, where human beings perceive and fully affirm the holiness of creation. This is not to deny that an individual could do this on her own, or in another (non-Christian) worshipping community. But it is to assert that creating a sacramental culture is one of the essential functions of the Church, and one that sets it at odds, or ought to at least, with the culture of secularism. Worship is based upon and consolidates a sacramentalist anthropology and ontology that is antithetical to that promulgated by most secular authorities, in particular the high priests of the mental health religion.

(The capacity to love atrophies very quickly in psychiatric facilities, and it is almost impossible to maintain there a sense of the holiness of the world.)

Second, in Orthodox Christianity worship takes on a particular form in accord with the Gospel and Holy Tradition. Father Alexander Schmemann has emphasized that the Eucharist is the center and source of the entire liturgical life of the authentic Church. "In the Eucharist the Church accomplishes the passage from this world into the world to come, into the eschaton; participates in the ascension of its Lord and in His messianic banquet, tastes of the joy and the peace of the Kingdom."[393] Schmemann has stated that the degree to which the Church actualizes Herself, "She embodies in worship Her participation in God's Kingdom."[394] Thus Christian worship, unlike other modes of worship, ideally rehearses and prepares individuals for the *parousia* and for the coming reign of the God of Israel.

Third, the Church must be aware of its own limitations as a culture. While in the "private" realm one may actualize Christian values, one may experience the sacramental quality of the world, one may love one's neighbor as oneself, yet in the "public" realm it is the law of the jungle that is the norm. The munitions industry, the multinational corporations with their unlimited supply of cheap labor under substandard conditions, the prisons, the lunatic asylums, the shopping malls, the legislative bodies influenced by corporate pressures—these are the institutions that dominate public life.

393 Father Alexander Schmemann, *Church, World, Mission* (Crestwood, New York: St. Vladimir's Seminary Press, 1979), p. 212.
394 Schmemann, *Introduction to Liturgical Theology*, (London: Faith Press, 1966), p. 23.

CHAPTER FOURTEEN

Because the capacity for love can only be potentiated when the structures of the world conform to Orthodox Christian standards, the Church must be both an "alternative society" and a transformative example, as Charles Scriven has put it. It must be "an agent of social conversion.... It must always confront the dominant ethos with the higher ethos of the Kingdom: it must always seek transformation."[395] Thus, the second way besides worship in which the Church fulfills its messianic function is to act as a transformative force in the world, so that various human structures and institutions become channels for the grace of God.

Worship must be complemented by service and by mission. In fact, as Schmenmann notes, worship and mission in both the monastic life and in the world are integrally connected. "The early Christians realized that in order to become the temple of the Holy Spirit they must ascend to heaven where Christ has ascended [as they can in worship]. They realized also that this ascension was the very condition of their mission in the world, or their ministry to the world. For there—in heaven—they were immersed in the new life of the Kingdom and when...they returned into the world their faces reflected the light, the joy and peace of that Kingdom and they were truly its witnesses....Wherever they went the seeds of the Kingdom sprouted....Things impossible were made possible."[396]

From the Orthodox perspective the Church as the Body of Christ is the instrument of God's purpose, called

395 Charles Scriven, *The Transformation of Culture* (Scottdale, Pennsylvania: Herald Press, 1988), p. 180.

396 Alexander Schmemann, *For the Life of the World* (Crestwood, New York: St. Vladimir's Seminary Press, 1973), p. 28.

upon to "actualize and manifest in the world the Kingdom of Heaven on earth."[397]

> The essence of the fallen world is that division, the separation of each from all, reigns in it. This is not overcome by the "natural" love of certain people for certain others, and it triumphs and is fulfilled by the ultimate "separation"—death.[398]

If the dominion of love is to replace the dominion of death as the principle of social life, i.e., if the principle of unity is to replace the principle of division, then the Church must seek to remove political as well as spiritual obstacles to the actualization of Christian norms. As Vladimir Solovyov wrote:

> The idea of the Kingdom of God necessarily brings us to the duty of doing what we can for realizing Christian principles in the collective life of mankind, and transforming all our social institutions and relations in the spirit of the higher truth....If as the champions of pseudo-Christian individualism assert, all social and political institutions are alien and even contrary to Christianity, true Christians ought to live without any such institutions. But this is an obvious absurdity disproved by their life and activity. If, however, social and political forms of life cannot be abolished (for that would be equivalent to abolishing man as a social and political being), and if on the other hand, they are as yet far from embodying Christian principles, it clearly follows that the task of Christian politics is to perfect

397 Ibid., p. 211.
398 Schmemann, *The Eucharist* (Crestwood, New York: St. Vladimir's Seminary Press, 1988), p. 137.

these forms and transmute them into realities fit for the Kingdom of God.[399]

The Church belongs to the New Aeon and thus transcends potentially the parameters of the fallen world. Rodney Clapp has described the Church as a "new and unique culture" that is poised now at "the pivot point of world history."[400] The Church is thus not merely a medium for the spiritual growth of individual Christians, it is a catalyst for the growth of humanity as a species, which requires the removal of the *political* obstacles to the realization of Christian fellowship with all human beings.

There is thus an integral bond between *worship*, as the essential act in which the Church experiences communion with God, glimpses the age to come, and constitutes Herself as the Body of Christ, the agent of the new order, and *mission*, which consists in the sundry activities by which this community seeks to create the spiritual, social, and political preconditions for the consummation of God's plan for the redemption of all creation—including the prisoner, the beggar, the madman, and the earth herself.[401]

---

399 S.L. Frank, ed., *The Solovyov Anthology* (New York: Charles Scribner and Sons, 1950), pp. 49-50.

400 Rodney Clapp, *A Peculiar People* (Downers Grove, Illinois: InterVarsity Press, 1997), p. 89.

401 In this regard, let us not forget that the Church has also been called "the hospital of the soul." It is no coincidence that from its earliest history the Church, both in its monastic function and through its lay communities, has funded hospitals, sheltered orphans, given homes to repentant prostitutes, taken in the unwanted, and fought for social justice, from the abolition of slavery and abortion to the provision of rights for women and children under the law.

Books and Music
from Regina Orthodox Press

The Faith: *Understanding Orthodox Christianity—*
An Orthodox Catechism by Clark Carlton. $22.95

The Way: *What Every Protestant Should Know about*
the Orthodox Church by Clark Carlton. $22.95

Letters to Fr. Aristotle: *A Journey through Contempo-*
rary American Orthodoxy by Frank Schaeffer. $22.95

Dancing Alone: *The Quest for Orthodox Faith in the Age*
of False Religion by Frank Schaeffer. $20.00

Portofino—a novel by Frank Schaeffer. The hilarious
adventures of a boy raised by Protestant missionaries. $6.99

First Fruits—At last, authentic Byzantine chant in English!
Boston Byzantine Choir. (1 hr., Music CD) $19.95

40% discount for orders of 5 or more books or CD's!

Please add 10% for shipping and handling. Foreign orders add 20%.
Massachusetts residents add 5% sales tax. All orders must be accompanied
by payment in U.S. funds or credit card information, including expiration
date.

REGINA
Orthodox Press
P.O. Box 5288
Salisbury, MA 01952

To Order Call Toll-Free (800) 636-2470
or Fax (978) 462-5079 with credit card information.

Videos
by Frank Schaeffer

My Personal Journey to Orthodoxy —A revealing personal account of conversion. (1.5 hrs., 1 VHS tape) $19.95

Orthodox Evangelism—What it is and how to practice it. (2 hrs., 2 VHS tapes) $29.90

The Defense of Orthodoxy—The classic introduction to Orthodoxy for inquirers. (5.5 hrs., 3 VHS tapes) $59.85

The True State of the Union—An Orthodox examination of the true state of our moral culture. (2 hrs., 1 VHS tape) $19.95

30% discount for orders of 4 or more video sets!

Please add 10% for shipping and handling. Foreign orders add 20%. Massachusetts residents add 5% sales tax. All orders must be accompanied by payment in U.S. funds or credit card information, including expiration date.

REGINA
Orthodox Press
P.O. Box 5288
Salisbury, MA 01952

To Order Call Toll-Free (800) 636-2470
or Fax (978) 462-5079 with credit card information.